Liam Hudson was educated at Whitgift School and Exeter College, Oxford, where he studied first modern history and then philosophy and psychology. In 1957 he moved to Cambridge, and took his Ph.D at the Psychological Laboratory four years later. In 1964 he became Director of the Research Unit of Intellectual Development at Cambridge and two years later was made a Fellow of King's College. In 1968 he moved to Edinburgh to the Chair of Educational Sciences. From 1974–5 he was a Member of the Institute for Advanced Study, Princeton. He is the author of three earlier books, *Contrary Imaginations* (1966), *Frames of Mind* (1968) and *The Cult of the Fact* (1972), and has edited a fourth, *The Ecology of Human Intelligence* (1970).

Liam Hudson

Human Beings

An Introduction to the Psychology of Human Experience

TRIAD PALADIN

Published in 1978 by Triad/Paladin Books
Frogmore, St Albans, Herts AL2 2NF

ISBN 0 586 08355 3

Triad Paperbacks Ltd is an imprint of
Chatto, Bodley Head & Jonathan Cape Ltd
and Granada Publishing Ltd

First published in Great Britain by
Jonathan Cape Ltd 1975
Copyright © Liam Hudson 1975

Made and printed in Great Britain by
Richard Clay (The Chaucer Press) Ltd
Bungay, Suffolk
Set in Monotype Ehrhardt

Contents

Illustrations

Acknowledgments

Anyone who sets out, as I have here, to describe his view of the subject in which he works, has more debts than he can possibly acknowledge: to those who taught him; to friends and contemporaries; to students and ex-students; to authors, many of whom he has not met; and to those generous spirits who have dropped ideas in his path, which he subsequently picks up and cherishes as his own. My only course, I feel, is to admit the profundity of these debts; to express my gratitude; but to attempt to mention by name only those who have helped me with the practical business of putting this book together: my wife Bernadine Jacot, Jane Berkoff, James McGuire, Val Mansfield, Alan Ravage, Peter Sheldrake, John Wolfers. They have offered suggestions, criticisms and moral support in abundance. The responsibility for the final product, though, remains entirely mine.

Institute for Advanced Study,   LIAM HUDSON
Princeton, New Jersey

October 1974

Part One

The Psychologist
and his Evidence

1 Where We Now Stand

This book is designed to serve as an introductory text; an invitation to approach the discipline of psychology in a certain way. The view of psychology it advances seems to me to have two virtues that more conventional approaches lack. It has immediate human relevance, in that it is about people and the lives they lead, rather than about rats or theories or statistics. And it is integrative, creating connections between traditions and styles of thought that have in the past been treated as separate: the artistic as well as the scientific; the biological as well as the cultural. For the heart of psychology lies, I believe, in interpretative argument: in the effort to make sense of what people think and do. And in establishing such interpretations, all sources of information and insight are acceptable: none is to be despised.

There is of course no way of requiring that psychologists should do work of human relevance, especially if their natural inclination is to avoid this. It does seem self-evident, though, that *some* of psychology ought to be about people; what is more, about those aspects of their own lives that people have themselves treated as vitally important. That, at least, is what this book attempts. I have focused on the territory that Freud defined in his phrase *Lieben und Arbeiten* – the spheres of love and work. I have done my best to knit together the evidence we now possess about these into a coherent story. But gaps and over-simplifications occur; and these are real in that they reflect the confusion that I have felt, and I think anyone must feel, when faced with evidence of what people are actually like. We are at times, after all, profoundly puzzling creatures.

The interpretative argument of such a psychology turns out to have three layers. There is, at the most primitive level, argument about evidence, and the patterns of inference that it can be used to support. This is the aspect of psychology that deals with the tactics and strategies of research, and is sometimes referred to as 'methodological'. It is a matter of nuts and bolts: humble perhaps, but indispensable – like plumbing. Lying above this there is the argument's second layer, the filling in the psychological sandwich: the level at which we think directly about human beings and how they work. It is here that we wonder why, say, one person takes risks while another is cautious; why one person is homosexual while another is heterosexual. We form interpretative hunches about them, and build theories. On top of this 'substantive' layer there lies a third. This is more philosophical in character. It is here that we worry about the more general assumptions about human experience that the psychologist makes: about the extent, for example, to which he sees people as responsible for what they do.

In terms of its organization, the text follows this sandwich pattern. The other chapters in Part 1 are mostly to do with tactics and strategies. They deal with the special characteristics of evidence about people; and with the down-to-earth problems of logic and inference. They also introduce some concepts vital to the rest of the book. Parts 2 and 3 – the filling – deal with what people themselves are like. Part 2 reviews some of our knowledge about the ways in which the mind works; while Part 3 looks at the question of human development – and does so, in part, as an extended example. Part 4 flows on from this but is more conceptual in tone. It rejects the materialistic view of human life that has so far dominated psychology; and sets up an alternative – one that allows the human imagination its place, and revolves around the paradoxes of individual freedom.

Such a text is bound to be selective. Psychology is by now a huge and rambling empire. And although much of what it includes is trivial, the requirements of space and coherence have forced me to leave some exciting areas of work largely out of account: early learning in children, for example, psychopharmacology, the study of neurosis. If the tone of the narrative is personal and biased, this is, I think, unavoidable. Objectivity remains a noble idea, and one we all strive towards, but research is in many respects an intensely personal business; and a book like this must ultimately stand or fall by the extent to which it makes this personal investment plain.

Necessarily, the portrayal of psychology offered here represents something of a break with the traditional view conveyed in textbooks: the conception of a scientific discipline unfolding with all the cumulative inevitability of a physical science. And to this extent, it is bound at moments to seem iconoclastic. The explanation of this lies in the very curious pattern of growth that twentieth-century psychology has followed.

Once upon a time, half a century ago, psychology was a subject of limitless promise. The founding fathers had done their work; and it must then have seemed that a coherent science of the mind was about to take shape. But what happened proved a disappointment. For while psychology grew immensely, in the United States especially, it split into rival schools of thought; most notably, the 'behaviouristic' and the 'psychoanalytic'. As a discipline, it has failed to evolve an agreed body of theory, or an agreed method. In practice, it amounts to no more than a ramshackle assemblage of topics, techniques and mutually incompatible points of view. And, more and more, the self-consciously scientific forms of psychology that have come to dominate university teaching departments have become artificial. Academic psychologists make studies of short-term memory; or people's abilities to shuffle cards; or their speed in response to flashing lights and buzzers. Or they settle for work on rats or pigeons.

Naïvely, one might expect psychologists to tell us why human beings think and feel and act as they do. This, after all, is the psychologists' 'historically constituted subject-matter'. But even when important-looking issues have been addressed, time and again these have been trivialized. In the course of a few years, for example, the discussion of human imagination and human intelligence has been reduced to the discussion of answers given by school-children to paper-and-pencil tests. Indeed, there is a proud tradition among us that the work we do should in no way resemble ideas about psychology that exist in the world at large. We study animal behaviour and we juggle with statistics. But none of this bears on the needs and deeds of ordinary men and women. For what professional psychologists pursue are not people, but the arcane rites of Science.

Such loftiness is not merely normal; it is *respectable*. To do research without relevance to the plain man and his lot is the hall-mark of the first-class mind. Work that makes gestures towards issues of human significance is seen as the preserve of the mediocre; while work that actually threatens to illuminate aspects of our lives that intimately concern us has been laughed off the academic stage as a fraud.[1]

Marxist critics have interpreted this flight from human sub-ject-matter as part of a capitalist plot; one aimed to distract students from the issues of power and control in the society that supports them. These critics are certainly right in pointing to the bizarre nature of what we now accept as normal. But to interpret the situation as a conspiracy is too simple. For what characterizes the militantly scientific in psychology is not simply their evan-gelical faith in the brave new world of science and technology; but their attack on the life of the mind.

During the 1920s and 1930s, a tide of sentiment seems to have swept over the United States and Great Britain, in favour of science and technology and hostile to introspection and the arts. It was a sentiment that favoured what William James has called 'tough-mindedness': the down-to-earth and matter-of-fact.[2]

Consequently, it has become the essence of the scientific tradi-tion in psychology that people should be considered as though they were complex *objects*. Systems that may or may not have problems. In a simple-minded way, it has become a refuge for the philistine and materialistic – those interested not in the finer shades of human thought or feeling, but in what people can be seen to *do*. What such psychologists seek to deny is that the in-dividual is systematically influenced by ideas; by events that take place in the mind. This attack has profound ethical implica-tions, which are well demonstrated, for example, in the popular writing of the latter-day American behaviourist, B. F. Skinner.[3] Skinner, whose experiments with rats and pigeons possess

1. A more detailed description of this academic Realpolitik is given in my earlier book *The Cult of the Fact* (1972). Full publication details of this and all other works cited are to be found in the reference section, pp. 193–204.
2. The history of academic psychology is still rather poorly documented. An account of our remoter origins is given by Boring (1942) and, on the psycho-analytic side, by Whyte (1962). Hearnshaw (1964) gives information about the scene in Britain; and there are useful contributions to the collection edited by Sexton and Misiak (1971). Chomsky (1970) has touched on the underlying issues of intellectual tradition, as do the articles in Wann (1964) and Mischel (1969). There remains, though, a great deal to do.
3. Skinner (1972).

genuine elegance and distinction, is impatient to move from pigeon evidence to human implication. By the standards either of common sense or of scholarship, inference from pigeon to man is slovenly. Yet, because Skinner invokes the authority of science, we have been led in the past to overlook the yawning gaps his arguments contain.

Recently, though, this quasi-religious vision of science has begun to fade. Suddenly we have grown more sceptical; and the academic salesmanship of the behaviourists is an accomplishment we now wish to probe. We find ourselves asking for evidence, and for close reasoning; and wondering too, about the motives of the salesmen themselves. And despite the attractions of lesser forms of wild-life, we are struck with the need to learn a little about ourselves.

Some time in the mid-1960s, and in a wide variety of places, thoughts were thought and articles written that three or four years earlier would have been unthinkable, unwriteable.[4] As prime sufferers of the infatuation with scientism, psychologists have perhaps experienced this shift of the *Zeitgeist* more dramatically than most. Those who used to expound the old virtues most strenuously, now have about them a slightly bewildered air. Too readily attracted towards the glamour of physical science, they overlooked what now seems obvious to almost all of us: the rich heartland of intuitive judgment, ethical assumption and personal commitment on which all forms of rational activity draw.

The present book is, then, part of an effort that many psychologists are making, on both sides of the Atlantic, to stitch psychology back into a coherent fabric. It rests on the daring assumption that psychologists should study the people around them. More than this, that we should scrutinize our work; our social, political and cultural loyalties; the lives we live in the privacy of our own homes; and the lives we live in the privacy of our own heads.

Psychology students have for generations been encouraged to see themselves as taking ruler and stop-watch to the world, measuring people with all the dispassion that they might show in recording the orbit of Jupiter, or the structure of a fruit-fly's wing. This self-image has been strengthened by our need for

4. One of the best of these is Kagan (1970).

academic respectability, as a fledgling profession; but it has led us to overlook the intuitive processes whereby we decide to collect one set of evidence rather than another, and place upon it one interpretation rather than another.

As we shall see, though, evidence about people is less determinate than evidence about animals, or about inanimate objects. If we are in the least interested in the rigour of what we do, we are forced to abandon the conception of ourselves as impersonal measurers, and to see ourselves more modestly as interpreters. Rather than granting ourselves a God-like exemption from the frailties we observe in others, we would be wise to begin with the picture of ourselves as ordinary: people doing their best to make sense of others, while they, simultaneously, do their best to make sense of us.

If we disavow the false objectivity that scientifically minded psychologists have claimed for themselves, we are still under no obligation to plunge to the other extreme. We can analyse and explore the elements of uncertainty that psychological knowledge contains without committing ourselves to a complete relativism of judgment, in which all interpretations of human thought or deed are ultimately of equal value. An interpreter works with evidence: he deals not in black or white, but in the subtly shifting and graduated shades of grey that reasoned doubt entails. His search, in practice, is always for the best reading that his evidence permits. His task is 'hermeneutic'; it is a species of systematic interpretation. And he himself is a 'hermeneut'.

As 'hermeneutic' is now in danger of becoming a mode word, this stress on evidence – on a 'text' – is worth bearing in mind; and so too are the distinctions between the three kinds of interpretative activity that the term can cover. There is, first of all, the classical usage, rooted in the German Biblical scholarship of the eighteenth century, in which the interpreter reconstructs another person's meaning, using that other person's concepts. There is the extended sense, exemplified by a psychoanalyst like Freud or an anthropologist like Lévi-Strauss, in which the reconstruction of meaning takes place in some new language – one that the person himself might well not recognize. And there is the third and altogether looser sense in which the 'text' is evidence of any sort that is being searched for a best reading. Psychology can be hermeneutic in all three of these senses. In other words, it is neither simply a science nor an art. To borrow a valuable category from the German language, it is a form of *Wissenschaft*: a pursuit of knowledge that draws on both the sciences and the arts, but lies somewhere in the mid-ground between the two. As such, it represents a search for forms of rigorous argument that have a genuine bearing on our human subject-matter. The shift is not from hard science towards soft and cosy subjectivity – from facts towards speculation – but from misplaced precision towards precision that is correctly applied.[5]

In the course of this search, the psychologist deals exclusively neither with thoughts nor with deeds; but with the interplay of the two. These two aspects of our experience, the private and the public, belong indispensably together; and it is on the flow from one to the other that our lives as individuals depend. In this context, it is worth reflecting for a moment on the pun hidden in this book's sub-title; specifically, the twin meanings of the phrase 'human experience'. For the thrust of behaviouristic psychology has split our conception of human experience in two. On the one hand, we are offered mental events; our private flicker show. On the other, the everyday wear and tear that constitutes our knowledge of the world and its workings. The first, we are persuaded, either does not exist or is trivial; while the second is too vague or messy to deserve rigorous analysis.

This bifurcation of our experience amounts to philosophical rape. To rip it apart is not simply to remove from the arena of discussion the meaning each of us perceives in the everyday life he leads. It is to conceive of psychology either as the technology of behaviour, or as a form of psychic sightseeing. The point about both approaches is that they encourage us to see the individual as *passive* – either as the victim of events that lie outside himself; or as a mere knot of sensations. In both cases, before our scrutiny begins, we strip the individual of his special status

5. See Wilhelm Dilthey's 'The Rise of Hermeneutics' (1972). Also helpful are Gardiner (1974), Geertz (1973) and Holt (1967). Implicit in the hermeneutic approach is an attack on two misconceptions of the scientific method, both of which have exerted a disastrous influence within psychology. The first is the 'inductive fallacy' – the assumption that laws will grow of their own accord out of evidence. The second is the 'hypothetico-deductive fallacy' – the assumption that evidence should be collected only as a means of supporting or rejecting deductions from formally stated hypotheses. It is an open question which of the two has generated the more barren research.

as an *agent*: someone who makes sense of himself and the world around him, and then acts in the light of the sense he makes.

To this extent, the psychologist must be willing to ally himself with the German nineteenth-century philosophical tradition of idealism, rather than accepting – as most of us unquestionably have – the tenets of British empiricism. For while the empiricists have envisaged the human mind as 'passively responding, in mechanical fashion, to the promptings of external or internal stimuli', the idealists portrayed it 'in predominantly active terms', treating it as 'creative and self-determining, playing a constructive role in life and experience'.[6] If we cannot grasp that our minds act in this integrative fashion, the serious work of psychological interpretation cannot begin.

In a three-lobed nutshell, this is a text about our capacity to make systematic sense of one another – about the game's more basic ground-rules, about the ideas we find it natural to use in playing it, and about the philosophical messages these ideas convey. If I am right, the real discipline of psychology lies in the vitality of the argument that the relations between these three lobes demand. We deal in evidence, but it must be evidence that is brought to life in the light of some broader imaginative plan. And the items of evidence we collect cannot just be materials that we use for or against a particular interpretation; richer than that, they must constitute the most penetrating account we can find of how people's lives are in fact conducted.

But this said, psychology remains, in the broadest sense, a philosophical activity. It is one of the few ways we have found in this century of expressing our sense of what human life is about. At every step, usually tacitly but occasionally more explicitly, the psychologist adjusts the boundary between appearances and reality: between what people seem to be, and what he claims they actually are.[7] Yet, to an extent that is only just dawning on us, we all make assumptions about human freedom and agency, about moral responsibility, about the 'realness' of the mind, about rationality, and about the nature of our access to other people's minds, that are philosophical. And in the very act of doing psychology, we also adopt attitudes about the nature of knowledge – and these are philosophical too.

6. Gardiner (1974), p. 4.
7. Hampshire (1969).

In the past, psychologists have seen themselves as creators of order, fixing people for all eternity within a framework of laws, like flies in amber. To adopt a distinction of Freud's that I shall use later on, their view of knowledge drew on the impulse to reduce the flux of living things to formality, and in this rather special sense was an expression of Thanatos, or the 'death instinct'. Presenting a carefully tailored front of objectivity to the world, they acted as though they were the impersonal instruments of some higher ethical system: the 'truth' that must be 'told'. Others, in rebellion against this pseudo-scientific view of psychology, have seen themselves more as facilitators: rather than interpreting or explaining, they have conceived of themselves as releasing whatever capacity for experience other people possess.

Both attitudes seem to me naïve. Here I shall steer a more central route. This is one in which conflicts of need and principle are envisaged as the most important activating force in each person's life, and in which the resulting tensions and ambiguities are seen not as problems to be resolved, but as the generative root from which all the most significant human accomplishments and transformations spring.

Until recently, academic psychologists have proceeded as though such issues of interpretative principle are best ignored and will, in some mysterious way, solve themselves or wither away. But to ignore them is to do our best to ensure the triviality of whatever research we undertake. Without a keen awareness of the alternatives open to us, both at the general conceptual level and at the technical one, our main task – that of making sense of people themselves, and of the changes their lives undergo – falters as soon as it has begun.

2 Evidence and Interpretation

At the centre of the psychologist's work there lies what has been called, perhaps a little melodramatically, the interpretative act: the intellectual activity whereby we knit together evidence and belief. We collect evidence in the light of our beliefs and hunches about people; and then turning back on ourselves, we use that evidence to refine – and eventually perhaps to refute – the positions from which we began. Neither evidence nor belief, we find, is of use to us in isolation; they draw their life and pertinence from the relation that springs up between them.

In an established science like physics, the manœuvrings between evidence and theoretical belief can take on a dignified, minuet-like pattern; and the understanding that emerges is cumulative. Problems are solved, and control of the world around is slowly (if sometimes regrettably) achieved. But in psychology, matters are altogether less clearly etched. In practice, the psychologists who make discoveries act more like detectives; detectives who search for clues.

What kind of evidence – what kind of clue – does the psychologist handle? The answer is a little awkward to frame, partly because psychological evidence is so diverse, and partly because it is an issue shrouded in superstition.

The diversity is real enough. We deal with what people do; with what people say they do; with what they say they think; and with what they say other people do and think. If we are shrewd, we also look at what we do and think ourselves. We may deal in case studies or big sample statistics. We may observe, like a fly on the wall; or we may intervene, conducting experiments. There is no stereotyped pattern for us to follow. At root, our evidence amounts to no more than a record of events that other people can properly trust.

Considered in bulk, evidence about people is of four kinds:

the biological, the cultural, the 'experiential', and the developmental. We are, first of all, creatures of flesh and bone; and the psychologist who ignores this fact does himself a disservice. The language of flesh and bone – of hormonal secretions, chromosomes and instincts – is that of the biologist. Just as unambiguously, we are also social, cultural entities. We have, each of us, an intimate environment: the parents, siblings, spouses, children, workmates, friends and enemies we deal with day by day, who provide the fabric of our daily lives. We have a broader cultural identity, too: the class and nation we belong to; the language we speak. These social and cultural aspects of our lives, again, we ignore at our peril. Yet in discussing such matters with sociologists, anthropologists and historians, we enter a world quite unlike that of the biologist. Here we speak of roles and expectations; traditions and classes; kinship and myth. And although biologists and social scientists employ arguments that overlap one with the other, they do so, for the most part, unawares. They live apart, usually in quite separate parts of their universities; and a light-year's distance from one another in terms of their assumptive worlds – the systems of belief about their subject-matter they find it natural to employ.

While the psychologist should take these two aspects of our knowledge about people into account, it is a third that offers him his own special stamping-ground. He draws on the separate, and often apparently incompatible wisdoms of the biologist and the social scientist. He does his best to integrate and reconcile. But the story he tells is not reducible, even in principle, to either of the other two. For if our interest is in people, we must come to terms with the mind and its contents. People are not impelled solely by the brute realities of biology and the social order; they are moved for most practical purposes, by their knowledge and beliefs, their desires and fears. It follows that the psychologist must think about thinking; he must come to terms with the idea of an idea. If he is to make sense of human experience, he must grasp the systems of *meaning* with which human thought and action are imbued.[1]

1. Far from being a matter of subjective leaps, this grasping of meanings is – as the hermeneutic tradition makes clear – a complex process of intellectual reconstruction. It is in my view compatible both with the search for causes, and with the desire to discover not veil on veil of appearances, but what is

Grossly inconvenient though it may be, human meanings are rarely the sorts of meaning that you find in a dictionary. They consist of attitudes and assumptions, beliefs and needs. Characteristically, such sentiments lie at least half-buried in the mind of the person under their influence. And quite often, especially when they are shameful, their owner will systematically deceive himself (and others) about their nature and strength. The contents of our minds are in these respects quite unlike our more presentable public products: the books we write, the cities we build, the music we compose, the computers we programme. Ideas are potent, and the paths they follow are, we assume, lawful; but the life of the mind is not made up of neat and tidy parcels, each with its label attached.

The psychologist's task is made more subtle by the passage of time. We do not spring into the world as fully-fledged individuals overnight; we develop. The experiences that shape us are cumulative, and the ideas that guide us from the cradle to the grave crystallize in our minds only slowly. We are subject, too, both to slow ground swells of change and to the occasional catastrophic upheaval. What we look forward to, what we remember and what we dread change as we grow up and grow old.

Taken together, our four types of evidence – the biological, cultural, experiential and developmental – could be said to form a prism, the psychologist's special interest lying on the surface of the prism that the experiential and the developmental edges define. His concern is with the growth and change of human experience through a lifetime. In more down-to-earth terms, his job is to make sense of people's biographies. And it requires little imagination to see that all four kinds of information interact, one with the other. The biological influences impinging on a young man differ from those that will impinge when he is old. Likewise with his cultural and social context. The society in which he lives, and the people among whom he moves, are continually changing. They do so, on a grand scale, through the historical and political evolution of his culture, as well as more prosaically, in terms of the faces he sees around him each day.

_____

actually going on. To abandon either of these quite basic aspects of systematic inquiry in the name of cultural relativism is to commit an enervating mistake.

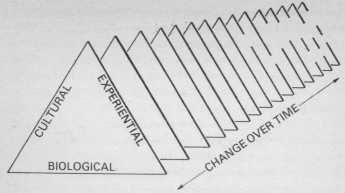

Figure 1. The 'prism' – the four types of evidence about the individual

Before we consider some niceties of psychological evidence, there are two superstitions surrounding this question that we can scotch. The first is a red herring we owe to the behaviourists. In 1913, J. B. Watson, an American animal psychologist of no very great distinction, proclaimed that we must in future concern our-selves only with 'stimulus' and 'response'; and that all talk of ideas must be banned – including, of course, any critical examina-tion of those ideas that inspired Watson.[2] The message fell on receptive ears: introspective psychology was at that time in difficulties; and people, in any case, had begun to feel the mag-netic tug of the metaphor of Man as Machine.

In the event, it proves impossible to move from the analysis of human utterance as the expellation of noise and warm, moist air to pertinent discussion of any sort at all. Though this self-denying ordinance of Watson's has now been largely abandoned, the suspicion still lingers that there is something vaguely im-proper – possibly even licentious – about the mention of ideas and their meaning. In particular, many of us still cling to the belief that what people say they do is more trustworthy than what they say they think.

Take, as an example, Kinsey's famous studies of human sex-uality; research usually accepted, despite its risqué subject-matter, as a contribution to orthodox science.[3] Kinsey's interest

2. Watson (1913). It is fitting that a polemicist like Watson should leave academic life and make a second career for himself in advertising.
3. Kinsey *et al.* (1948), (1953).

lay in cataloguing our sexual 'outlets'. He asked thousands of men and women to describe what they had done, and with whom. Also, more peripherally, he made a study of sexual fantasies. What we should notice is the confidence that the two sorts of evidence have inspired. When Kinsey reports that a certain lawyer had maintained an average of between 25·6 and 37·8 orgasms a week over a period of thirty years, we tend to treat this as a 'fact', acceptable at its face value. When he records that another individual experienced fantasies of flagellation, we are more sceptical, and wonder whether this can really be a 'fact' at all. But the first fact is in all probability less trustworthy, more fragile, than the second. Few of us can remember what we did thirty years ago, especially in a realm as uncertain as that of sex; and diaries are by no means reliable. In recollection, the spontaneous distortions of memory are likely to be formidable. Kinsey's lawyer could well have been a profoundly self-deceptive raconteur. There is no reason, on the other hand, why Kinsey's questions about people's current sexual fantasies, if asked with sufficient care, should not have generated data that are very trustworthy indeed.

In short, it is not the 'mental-ness' or the 'physical-ness' of events that governs whether or not they should inspire our trust. Rather, the extent to which our records of them are open to systematic distortion, either by the observer or by the observed.

Kinsey's work touches on our superstitions in a second way. He was a man who made his reputation by counting literally millions of gall wasps. He fortified that reputation by counting other people's recollections of their orgasms. Again, millions of them. And his work is accepted as orthodox, partly because it is expressed numerically, the form of presentation distracting us from the thousands of smudgy human judgments from which his statistics derive. Psychology, more generally, has made something of a fetish of numbers. We are taught that we must have a sample that is 'large enough'; that our findings are best cast up in the form of tables and diagrams. Some of the research described in this book takes this form; often enough, the conventions are helpful. Nevertheless, over the last half century, academic psychologists have conspicuously neglected the form of inquiry that has so often led to insight in other fields: namely, the meticulous study of the individual case.

Fastidiously used, statistics are a powerful aid to certain sorts of analysis; but employed as a matter of partially comprehended routine, they serve the altogether disastrous function of insulating the psychologist from his subject-matter. And, as in other forms of craft, making furniture, for example, and pottery, mechanical aids and poor design seem to have advanced hand in hand. Almost certainly, psychologists have perpetrated more pointless research over the last ten years, with the aid of computers, than the human race has achieved in the whole of its previous history. The reason, no doubt, is the familiar one: that, like the rest of human kind, we follow any path that relieves the pain of thought.

Think, though, we must: among much else, about those respects in which evidence about people is unlike evidence about objects. Three areas of uncertainty, or indeterminacy, concern us particularly. Each is inescapable. We may call them the problems of 'embedding', of 'self-deception' and of 'feed-back'.

Ideas draw their weight and propulsive power from the situations with which each of us is forced to cope. We say of a person that the meanings he perceives are 'embedded' in the contexts that surround him. To put the matter crudely, the idea of a potato will have had one meaning to a starving Irish peasant in the mid-nineteenth century; and quite another to a well-nourished American advertising executive of the present day.

This phenomenon of contextual embedding places the psychologist on tricky ground. If he is to understand the meaning of what another person says, he must systematically reconstruct that person's context. If he is male, he must reconstruct the world as women see it. If he is American, he must reconstruct the world as it is seen by someone who is British, or French, or Egyptian. Whether the barriers are gross, as in the case of language, or matters more nearly of nuance, as with differences in class or education, psychology unavoidably becomes a 'cross-cultural' venture. But a trap awaits us. For it is the function of contexts not only to shape our ideas, but also to lend them an air of self-evident truth. They motivate, but they also blinker. It follows that if we share our neighbour's way of life, we share his blind spots too.

So, in attempting to bridge the gap between his own world of understanding and someone else's, the psychologist must, simultaneously, both share and remain distant. If he is a Jew attempting to understand an Arab, it is useless for him to judge solely from the standpoint of a Jew; but it would be equally pointless – were it possible – to try to turn himself completely into an Arab. He must, somehow, move to and fro in the mid-ground, attaining a grasp of both systems of understanding, but abstracting himself somewhat from both.[4]

A second source of indeterminacy in psychological explanation arises from the fourth edge of the prism – the passage of time. As poets, novelists and the occasional philosopher have reminded us down the centuries, it is man's nature endlessly to rewrite the past. The French writer Marcel Proust puts the position eloquently at the end of *Swann's Way*:

The reality that I had known no longer existed . . . The places that we have known belong now only to the little world of space on which we map them for our own convenience. None of them was ever more than a thin slice, held between the contiguous impressions that composed our life at that time; remembrance of a particular form is but regret for a particular moment; and houses, roads, avenues are as fugitive, alas, as the years.[5]

Quite simply, the psychologist's target is a moving one; and, as human as anyone else, he moves too. At first sight, the point seems familiar: it reminds us of those textbook illustrations of Einstein's principle of relativity. But it is more elusive than that. For, in representing events to ourselves, we all – plain men and psychologists alike – protect ourselves systematically from truths that are too painful or inconvenient to bear.

Our vision is not just selective. It can also become – and, some would say, always is – systematically self-deceptive. So it is not enough for the psychologist to construe another's experience as that other person construes it; he must construe in the light of evidence about what actually occurs. Let us say that Mr X believes he is a loving husband, but quarrels with his wife, and is persistently secretly unfaithful to her. It simply will not do, as a

---

4. Arguably, he may be able to *broaden* his perspective; but as he does so, he risks a loss of vitality. As with international organizations, so with individuals: the end-product is usually dispiritingly bland.
5. Proust (1966), p. 288.

piece of psychological research, to accept Mr X's perception of himself at its face value. Obviously, he differs from Mr Y, who holds the same belief about himself, but who does not quarrel, and is not unfaithful.

We need little imagination to see how fine drawn our interpretative task can become. What, for example, of Mr P, who believes he loves his wife, who is not unfaithful to her, but who privately wishes he could be? Or Mr Q, who is unfaithful neither in thought nor deed, yet whose protestations of love for Mrs Q ring hollow?

Clearly, such self-deceptions and dissociations do not occur solely for personal reasons. They can serve social and political ends too.[6] What is more, the cultural context in which our experience is embedded may have such dissociations built into its very fibres. One can argue, perfectly plausibly, that it is the nature of cultural systems to create dissociations: that it is only through the creation of these that the people who live within them have any form of self-expression at all. The argument is an impressive one; and although the psychologist need not make doctrinaire assumptions about it, he must be wary. Some dissociations of sensibility or action may be a personal matter, local to the individual. But in choosing between styles of life, a person may frequently be choosing, not between better and worse, but between one system of cultural convention and another – each emotionally dissociating in its own way.

We begin to grasp the true delicacy of the psychologist's position as an interpreter when we see that his own interpretations become part of the cultural diet on which the people he studies feed. The ideas he develops about what is 'normal' or 'abnormal' become part of the cultural brew. Beyond serious question, Freud's writing has exerted just such an influence. When the psychologist publishes, he muddies the pool; or, rather, he stirs the mud already in that pool into new whirls and eddies.

As Jules Henry has rather sourly remarked, while 'dogs are bound by biology, humans can soar on the wings of conventionalized misrepresentation'.[7] Where his fellow humans soar, the psychologist must dutifully follow. He must also take note, as he

6. Szasz (1962a), Laing (1967).
7. Henry (1966), p. 273.

does so, of the conventionalized misrepresentations on which he likewise is soaring. The 'intelligence quotient', 'Oedipus complex', the idea of 'conditioning', are all three psychological ideas in wide currency. All three have changed our view of ourselves in ways as profound as they are unexamined.

Scientists tell us that they are people who spend their time telling stories, and then testing them rigorously to see if they are stories about real life.[8] In this rather liberal sense of the term, the psychologist is – and ought to be – a scientist too.

Yet we have it on Einstein's authority that there exists no path that 'leads from experiment to the birth of a theory'.[9] The incubation of insights, the formulation of theories, is work for the imagination. And in searching for an explanation, we fall back over and again on our own personal stock of visual images, metaphors, similes. Trying to grasp how the brain works, we liken it to a telephone exchange or a computer. And in the process, we develop loyalties to particular families of metaphors: behavioural psychologists, for example, show a strong taste for mechanical and electronic imagery, while psychoanalysts have tended to turn towards that of domestic architecture and plumbing.

In this respect, as in any other, our loyalties tend to imprison us – and especially so if we are ashamed to admit that we use metaphorical thought at all. In a prescient essay, the American psychologist Jerome Bruner has pointed in this context, to the pregnant symbolism of our left and right hands, and to the parallel between these and our two complementary modes of grasping reality – the intuitive and the more explicitly rational:

Reaching for knowledge with the right hand is science. Yet to say only that much of science is to overlook one of its excitements, for the great hypotheses of science are gifts carried in the left . . .

And should we say that reaching for knowledge with the left hand is art? Again it is not enough, for . . . there is a barrier between undisciplined fantasy and art. To climb the barrier requires a right hand adept at technique and artifice . . .

The psychologist, for all his apartness, is governed by the same constraints that shape the behaviour of those whom he studies. He too searches widely and metaphorically for his hunches . . . If he is not

8. Medawar (1967).
9. Vallantin (1954), p. 105.

fearful of these products of his own subjectivity, he will go so far as to tame the metaphors that have produced the hunches, tame them in the sense of shifting them from the left hand to the right hand by rendering them into notions that can be tested.[10]

The intimacy that exists between these two ways of knowing, the left- and the right-handed, forms part of the skeleton on which this book hangs. One of its guiding assumptions is that understanding human beings is a two-handed task; one that demands our highest manipulative skill.

If we are to grasp why psychologists of different schools disagree with one another so profoundly, and so personally, we must first disinter the metaphorical presuppositions on which each takes his stance. Only then can we begin to see how orderly compromises between schools of thought might be attained. Over the last hundred years, we have drawn overwhelmingly on the imagery of the Industrial Revolution: the internal combustion engine, the structure of steel girder and rivet. And this preponderance of technological imagery has encompassed all aspects of our thought: our attempts to explain specific aspects of human nature; our sense, more generally, of what it is to be 'scientific'; and our assumption that explaining human activity is synonymous with controlling it. Arguably, most eloquent of all has been the image of the bridge: the bridge over troubled waters. Scientific psychologists are 'bridge-builders' to a man; people who see themselves constructing fine steel arcs through space – safe thoroughfares across a landscape that is dangerously arbitrary and raw. Their conception of their own work is as pure a distillation as one could find of technological optimism.

In sharp contrast, there runs through psychology a quite different strain: the concept of man in a state of nature, before the Industrial Revolution began. Sometimes this expresses itself as a Rousseau-esque delight in the pastoral idyll: nymphs and shepherds fulfilling their natural functions. But as frequently it reflects the destructiveness of natural forces: the fire, flood and tempest. And many of the more profound disagreements that arise among psychologists seem reducible, in practice, to this conflict of latent imagery, the behaviourists building bridges over voids of ignorance, while the more psychodynamically inclined search for the well-springs that erupt from within. What

10. Bruner (1962), p. 2.

21

is more, reminiscent of the classical and romantic traditions in the nineteenth century, our thought seems naturally to polarize towards one or other of these conflicting views. Like rainwater on a pitched roof, psychological argument tends to gather in the guttering along either side.

3 Patterns of Inference

Whatever his broad interpretative presuppositions and pre-judices, the psychologist looks to his evidence; and this relation-ship with his data-base is an intimate one. For his evidence forms a kind of scaffolding; a structure that he builds up be-tween himself and those aspects of human nature he wants to examine. And placed in this way, it can serve either as a means of access, or, more destructively, as an obstacle. Continually, it 'answers back', forcing its begetter to abandon the comforting stereotypes into which his thinking slips, and requiring of him efforts of comprehension that he could not make of his own accord. Sometimes, when research is going well, this traffic with the data-base is apparently so reciprocal that one is tempted to borrow the pathetic fallacy from the poets, and to think of this as though it were a relation between one person and another. No doubt this is too fanciful; but the analogy does make it easier to grasp the extent to which bodies of evidence have lives of their own – as a source of excitement and inspiration, or as tyrannous, autonomous obstructions to the flow of insight. Only too easily we can establish the wrong data-base for our purposes, or employ the wrong methods of analysis upon it.

When he goes to his evidence, the psychologist is governed by precisely the same rules that govern all forms of orderly debate. These constrain him in the same way that they constrain the biologist, the lawyer, or the historian. On the other hand, it is hard to draw inferences from evidence, especially evidence about people, without disguising from yourself the assumptions im-plicit in your decision to collect and analyse your evidence in one way rather than in others. These hidden assumptions restrict the kinds of conclusion you reach; what is more – an awkward point to grasp – they can constitute the very models and metaphors of human life in terms of which your conclusions are conceived.

The aim of this chapter is to disentangle some of the more gratuitous knots that we have tied round ourselves in the search for a 'scientific method'; and to point out, more positively, what kinds of research design the study of human lives commits us to. The tone may seem unnecessarily carping, even the positive suggestions emerging in a rather roundabout and negative way. This I regret, but have lacked the expository skill to change. The difficulty arises, I suspect, partly because past errors are so tempting – and *should* be displayed, like gibbets on the heath, as reminders of where carelessness can lead. But also because, in argument about argument, it is always safer to attack mistakes than to make a positive recommendation. For there is no magic recipe: no right way of collecting evidence and drawing inferences from it. In psychology at least, it is more a matter of route-finding across an indeterminate space – one hedged around with pitfalls, and in which common sense and ingenuity are still our indispensable guides.[1]

First we should be clear that the process of analysing data, of knocking them into shape, is always something of a carnage. Even an investigator like Kinsey, who seems, to the point of tedium, to have reported everything and rejected nothing, in fact selects and orders ruthlessly. The reduction to averages of hundreds of thousands of individual reports about rates of sexual 'outlet' destroys almost everything of interest about those reports – unless, for the sake of a particular argument, it is the average you happen to need.

Characteristically, psychologists butcher even more vigorously than this. Whole tracts of evidence we omit altogether as boring or irrelevant. Where we bring out a particular effect, either statistically, or by means of case material, we automatically omit much of the evidence that would be crucial to other, rival interpretations: ones we dislike or have not thought of. Anyone who has collected and marshalled evidence knows this to be true.

The number of rival interpretations you can place on a given body of evidence is in principle limitless. What matters in practice is that the interpretation you offer should be a 'good' one. It should pick out aspects of the material that seem pertinent. It

1. Unfortunately, there are few worthwhile texts on methodology, perhaps because most are written by people who do not themselves do good research. An exception is Webb *et al.* (1966).

should be accurate, internally consistent, and, if possible, intelligible. It should also have a bearing on the broader framework of ideas that has sprung up around the field in question; and it should lead to new evidence, new discoveries. It is not enough simply to produce a story that is *compatible* with the evidence – a story that is usually, in effect, an extension of its teller's bountiful ego. It must constitute the *best* reading – the reading that captures most succinctly what the evidence has to say.[2]

In practice, day to day, the vital distinction is that between interpretations which are fertile, and those which are trivial or barren. This, it need hardly be said, is not wholly an objective matter; rather, one of judgment. That is to say, one on which differences of intelligence, temperament, tradition, fashion and the state of the immersing culture all have a bearing. It is the kind of issue over which some of us are consistently more perceptive than others.

Many psychologists who acknowledge that these problems of selection and judgment exist, none the less believe that all such awkwardnesses end once the impersonal processes of statistical analysis begin. Nothing could be further from the truth.

In a recent article on the application of mathematics to the biological and social sciences, the mathematician Zeeman points out that since Newton invented the calculus, the main tool for the application of mathematics has been the differential equation. Valuable in the physical sciences, this branch of mathematics has been carried over quite uncritically into biology, psychology, sociology and economics. There, Zeeman argues, quite different models are required – not because biological and social processes are hopelessly complex, but because they are more susceptible to abrupt change:

2. The question of what distinguishes a good interpretation from a poor one remains deep and difficult. To some extent it must depend on a social consensus; and to some extent, pragmatically, on whether a particular interpretation 'works' – whether it enables us to adapt successfully to our environment. There is a problem, though, about interpretations that are 'paranoid' – over-inclusive, and impervious to contrary evidence; and, in any case, the consensual and pragmatic justifications are in themselves quite inadequate. Like an elephant, a good interpretation is something that most of us recognize when it is placed in front of us. But for the moment, a formal account of this vital human skill eludes us. A helpful source in this context is Habermas (1972).

Gradual changes in environment may cause sudden evolutionary changes, or sudden cultural advances or sudden changes of opinion. People suddenly change their minds, and suddenly lose their temper, and suddenly burst into tears. Nations suddenly go to war. The smoothly growing embryo suddenly begins to fold . . .[3]

Zeeman's point is that while such phenomena do not fit the statistical models we are now using, they are compatible with certain models drawn from topological geometry, like the 'cusp catastrophe'; ones well suited to predict the sudden switches in response of a system subject to increasing but conflicting pressures or demands.

Zeeman's criticism cuts deep; for few psychologists at present using statistics fully understand the more basic logical assumptions on which their routine statistical techniques rest. And it will not have occurred to one in a thousand that the whole branch of applied mathematics on which we so trustingly perch may prove to be the wrong branch. Yet not only may an inappropriate mathematical model cause orderly behaviour to look confused and indeterminate; it may lead us to shy away from interesting aspects of behaviour, because they look too awkward to handle. Reviewing the routine statistical manoeuvres employed in psychology, one certainly sees a reluctance to entertain explanatory models that depend on sharp discontinuities: to use concepts like the brink, the threshold, or the boundary. Also a reluctance to use mathematical models as an aid in the clarification of our ideas. Where at present crude and inexplicit metaphors are shuffled together with insensitive data-handling techniques, there is surely a case for models that spell out some of the logical implications of the metaphorical language we use.

However, the psychologist's analytical assumptions are by no means restricted to his tacit models and his statistics. There are those, too, of research design. Let us begin a conducted tour of the pitfalls by looking at those that await the psychologist when he sets out to understand people in general by studying a few in particular; Freud, for instance. Some of the most exciting psychological research ever done has concentrated on small handfuls of individuals – people who are in one way or another remarkable. Men and women, that is to say, with spectacular

3. Zeeman (1971), p. 1556.

gifts; or who are in some respect crippled: the anxious, the half-mad.

We usually seek to imply that the mental processes displayed by such people are latent in all of us. The idea is a good one; but, as it stands, it is logically precarious. For the qualities we observe may be by-products of the unusual experiences of the people in question, not the shadow of a mental architecture that all human beings share. And even if such architecture were universal, the aspects of it relevant to us in extremity may tell us little about the aspects that influence us when our lives are more conventionally within bounds. We cannot make assumptions about an issue as basic as this. We must go and look.

An analogous trap awaits us whenever we decide to be more precise in the collection of our evidence; to devise experiments, and to measure. In either case, we almost invariably create situations that are artificial: intelligence-testing sessions, encounter groups, laboratory experiments. What people do for us there is 'real' enough. But we do not know, propped in our arm-chairs, to what extent such behaviour is characteristic of these men and women. Whether it is 'revealing', or merely 'artifactual'. Again, we need more evidence; and we should move with care.

Both these dangers – argument from the *abnormal*, and argument from the *artificial* – raise the more fundamental issue of generalization. Here, part of the argument is easy to see; part of it exceptionally slippery. We run into risk, patently, in moving from the particular to the more general. When Freud generalized about human nature on the strength of a tiny handful of late Victorian, middle-class, Jewish Viennese, he was arguing inductively. He was assuming that the laws governing human beings are the same the whole world over. Just as we all have eyes and ears, hearts and lungs, so are we all victims of Oedipal turmoil.

The attack on this assumption is easy; perhaps too easy. As anthropologists like Malinowski pointed out in the 1920s and 1930s, what holds for Viennese Jews does not necessarily hold for South Sea islanders; nor even, perhaps, for Viennese gentiles. What held in 1900 may not hold in 1970. What held for the middle class may not hold for the working class. And so on, *ad infinitum*. The hazards should not throw us into panic; but we would be fools to ignore them.

So far, so easy; the trap is so well signposted that few of us fall into it without at least half-realizing that we are doing so. Far more insidious, and far more damaging to psychology, are the various forms of nonsense that arise when psychologists move in the reverse direction, from the general to the particular.

Faced with a complicated body of evidence, almost all psychologists who are even marginally numerate begin by calculating correlations. The whole of the theory of mental measurement, for example, has this tactic at its root.[4] We look to see whether high scorers on one variable are high (or conspicuously low) scorers on others. Where we find agreement, we report these correlations as our findings. In practice, if the correlation between any two variables is high, we look more closely; if low, we ignore it.[5]

Research projects in their droves have followed this pattern; and, the while, their authors have almost always failed to notice the violence they are doing to common sense. For there is no reason, logical or psychological, why high correlations should interest the psychologist; nor why a low correlation should signify a relationship he can safely ignore. Correlation is one matter; psychological significance another. There are two sorts of reasons why this should be so. The first concerns people considered as a whole, the second the way in which each individual's life takes shape.

Quickly, let us clear the ground. A relation between two variables can be high, but of no interest. If we compare the length of men's big toes, left feet against right, the correlation will be high, but trivial. Conversely, there may exist no correlation between two variables, yet the interaction between them may none the less be of importance. The relationship may be non-linear: high scores on the first variable may go, let us say, with middling scores on the second variable; and low scores on the first with high scores on the second; and so on. Or, more urgent, the two variables may *combine* in their influence on the people we study;

4. See, for example, Guilford (1959) or Vernon (1961).
5. This is something of an over-simplification. Sometimes the psychologist will look for low correlations between two clusters of variables, each of which inter-correlate highly: as, for instance, in the case of tests of 'intelligence' and 'creativity' (Wallach and Kogan 1965). The assumption that a low correlation entails the absence of a significant psychological connection none the less holds.

and do so irrespective of whether the correlation between them is quite high, middling, or non-existent.

In one of the first pieces of research I ever undertook, I gave some psychological tests to a group of students in the humanities, some of whom, academically speaking, were doing quite exceptionally well.[6] It turned out that their I.Q.s differed greatly; and so too did the width of their reading, and how hard they worked. The inter-correlations between these three variables were, effectively, nil. I noticed, though, that among the most successful each student was *either* high in I.Q., *or* very widely read, *or* exceptionally hard-working. These three qualities, in other words, represented three different survival strategies. Only if he lacked all three of these qualities was a student in academic difficulties. The three variables were functional equivalents, combining in their relation to the further variable of academic success.

Such combinatory patterns crop up repeatedly. As a more formal statement of the same relationship, look at Figure 2A overleaf. The scores for each of twenty people on two variables – ambitiousness and radicalism – are plotted one against the other. (One of these twenty hypothetical people is William Truelove.) A quick glance at the scatter diagram shows that the two variables are not correlated: there are as many ambitious radicals like William Truelove as there are unambitious ones. Similarly with the conservatives.

The normal response to such a result is that the analysis has not worked. But if, in Figure 2B, we now make exactly the same plots on our scatter diagram, and instead of representing each person with an 'x', we do so with his score on a third variable, showing whether he is mentally flexible (F) or mentally rigid (R), the change is remarkable. The ambitious radicals and un-ambitious conservatives both prove to be flexible; the un-ambitious radicals and the ambitious conservatives turn out to be rigid. So although unrelated when considered in isolation, 'conservative/radical' and 'ambitious/unambitious' are variables that do combine lawfully after all – in terms of their relation to the third variable, 'flexible/rigid'.

Although the prospect of handling more than four or five such

6. Hudson (1961).

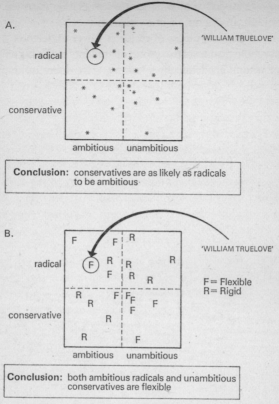

A.

radical

conservative

ambitious   unambitious

'WILLIAM TRUELOVE'

Conclusion: conservatives are as likely as radicals to be ambitious

B.

radical

conservative

ambitious   unambitious

'WILLIAM TRUELOVE'

F = Flexible
R = Rigid

Conclusion: both ambitious radicals and unambitious conservatives are flexible

Figure 2. Hidden correlations: a hypothetical example

variables in combination is statistically daunting, there is no reason why combinatory patterns should not be a standard feature of the mind's operation.

Still more alarming, statistically speaking, is the problem's second facet: that of human individuality. Although most of us may be said, within broad limits, to run 'true to type', the diverse elements of each person's biography combine to form patterns that are, at least in detail, uniquely his own. We each embody a 'specification': qualities like our radicalism, or flexibility, or ambitiousness, which may or may not express themselves consistently. Figure 3 shows some of William Truelove's qualities; the rudiments of his 'specification'. The broad outline

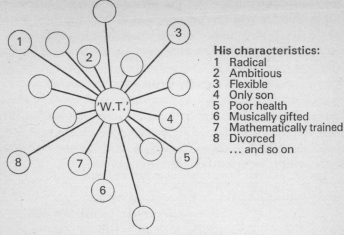

His characteristics:
1 Radical
2 Ambitious
3 Flexible
4 Only son
5 Poor health
6 Musically gifted
7 Mathematically trained
8 Divorced
... and so on

Figure 3. 'William Truelove's' specification

of the pattern is one he would share with quite a large number of people; but in detail it is his alone.

However, like everyone else, William's life is shaped by events: the death of a parent, an early marriage, a traffic accident, a lucky and influential meeting, a long-drawn-out illness, a war. Some of the salient events in William's life are shown, using a time scale, in Figure 4. Again, the broad outline is one that quite a number of people share; but, in matters of detail, the sequence is unique.

But a person is not simply a conglomerate of qualities and events. His mind is governed by certain preoccupations, which may well change from one phase of his life to another. It is these central preoccupations that form what existentialists like Sartre

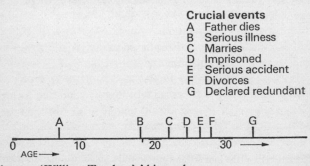

Crucial events
A Father dies
B Serious illness
C Marries
D Imprisoned
E Serious accident
F Divorces
G Declared redundant

Figure 4. 'William Truelove's' biography

somewhat ambiguously call the person's 'project'. Figure 5 shows that in William Truelove's case there are four such phases: a youthful preoccupation with school work; followed, in early adulthood, by his love for Anne Sparrow; displaced, in its turn, by a passionate involvement in politics; displaced, in his early thirties by a new mood of doubt about 'life' and its 'meaning'. Now thirty-four, William may soon make some new discovery about himself: that he was never at heart a mathematician, say, but a businessman; or that his political instincts are at root conservative, not revolutionary; or that, his marriage notwithstanding, he is in truth a homosexual.

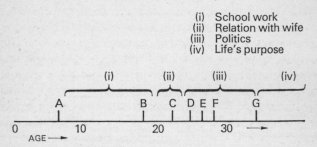

Figure 5. 'William Truelove's' changing preoccupations

The issue to be grasped is that each person's biography, his experience, is the outcome of an interaction between his 'specification', on the one hand, and the events and preoccupations of his life on the other. In diagrammatic terms, William Truelove's biography springs from the interplay between Figures 3, 4 and 5. The psychologist's prime task is to discover the rules that such an interplay observes.[7]

Between them, Figures 2 to 5 represent a chain, linking the general to the particular. It is one that we know how to break into, point by point; but which permits no safe inference in either direction. You can infer nothing about Figures 4 or 5 on the basis of Figures 2 or 3; nor vice versa. Likewise, you can infer nothing about Figure 3 on the basis of any of the others. Each, we must build for ourselves.

7. The strength of the interaction between traits and situations has been remarked on frequently: for instance by Bowers (1973).

It is sobering to reflect that while massive efforts have in the past been made along the path of Figure 2, little has been expended on the other possibilities; nor on the relations between them. Yet, if we were forced to choose, it is almost certainly the detailed study of the individual life that will most quickly advance our systematic knowledge. The movement between general interpretative concepts and statistical evidence about groups, in contrast, offers shakier insights, more tenuous verification, and a thicket of extra inferential puzzles.[8]

Whole generations of psychologists, for example, have persuaded themselves that the key to our powers of thought lies in 'g', the general intelligence factor; this being the blurred average that emerges from the intercorrelations of hundreds of tests given to millions of people. Yet armed with William Truelove's score on this dimension, we can conclude virtually nothing about his mental life. It will tell us roughly how bright he is compared with his fellows; but beyond that, we have everything to learn: whether he has any special flair, for instance for music or mechanics; whether he is eager to learn or happy to bumble along; whether we can help him to think more efficiently – and whether he would be co-operative if we tried. It does not even tell us if he is fast and slipshod, or accurate but slow; if he is logical or imaginative; or if his bias is towards words or towards numbers.

Implicit in this approach to evidence is the assumption – an irrational one – that if people's responses do not run true to type across a wide range of contexts, those responses are in some undisclosed sense 'random'. Yet we know, on grounds of common sense, that responses are often 'situation-specific'. A young man may have, say, an exclusive passion for hi-fi electronics. If we approach him bearing a broad assortment of mental tests, we are almost bound to miss the set of issues round which his world rotates. If we take his answers on these tests and pool them into 'scores' – a verbal score, a numerical score, and so on – we systematically obscure the focus of his interest; and learn nothing,

8. A sound routine procedure is to build up samples, one at a time, from individuals, each of whom has been studied in detail. And preferably to do so gradually, so that an articulated pattern of inference has time to evolve. Stoller's (1968) work on sex and gender, discussed in Chapter 8, is an instance of this.

within that field of focus, about how skilled he has become. In other words, once someone's interests and commitments have crystallized, we can only appraise him by entering his field of interest and commitment. In the case of the young electronics wizard, there is nothing for it: the psychologist must find some way of judging how skilled this young man is in the branch of electronics that particularly absorbs him.

If the psychologist must be wary of the assumptions that underlie a neat-looking test score, he must positively bristle with caution in its practical application. Granted that someone – our young electronics enthusiast, or a black child, or a working-class adult – scores rather poorly on our tests, what have we learnt? As yet, very little. The tests may accurately reflect his capabilities; they may not. And inasmuch as we have the power to influence that person's life using our scores, what effect will we have? In all probability, mischief of the most regrettable kind; especially if we imply that his scores represent his 'general mental ability' or 'intelligence'. For, in doing this, we assume that each person applies himself with the same dedication and skill to all tasks, irrespective of whether or not they possess for him any real meaning.

It is at this point that what appears, at first sight, to be a purely statistical issue slips over into one of covert ideology. For what we are saying, in effect, is that people *ought* to apply themselves with solemn dedication to our tests. Conversely, that there is something 'maladaptive' about them if they cannot focus themselves as we deem appropriate.

Surreptitious inferences creep into our work by another route. Correctly, we worry that any one of our results may have arisen from a coincidence or fluke. The game of probing other people's research, looking for trivial or boring explanations of what they believe to be exciting findings is known as 'nothing buttery'; and very enjoyable it can be.

The game's ground-rules are ones, however, about which we are at present doing some heart-searching. We have been brought up to believe that our measurements must be 'statistically significant', 'reliable' and open to 'replication'. They must be 'significant' – they must reflect an improvement over the results we might expect by chance. They must be 'reliable' – we must be able to repeat them consistently. And they must be open to 'replication' – we must be able to repeat, not just single measurements, but the whole study, again and again, on different groups of people, and get the same result.

Sensible enough, you would have thought; but on this foundation we have managed to erect a veritable citadel of misconception. For decades, psychologists have applied tests of statistical significance, like the 'chi-squared' test, as a matter of routine.[9] There is now great uncertainty, though, as to when such procedures can correctly be applied. Sometimes, when you are doing a piece of research, it helps, as a rein on premature enthusiasm, to know what a random set of results would look like. The resemblance with your own is often startling. But, characteristically, human beings do not act randomly; psychologists do not collect their samples randomly; and psychologists do not apply tests of statistical significance randomly to their results – only to their best ones. So, *de rigueur* until recently, tests of significance are now falling out of favour. As often as not, they are retained from sheer force of habit; or because we can think of no other way of making our results look scientific.

This is a technical matter. Of greater practical concern are the consequences of the search for reliability and replication. We tell ourselves that results based on one sample should be repeatable on others. People, however, are not rows of beans. Or, rather, they are more like rows of beans in some respects than in others. In dealing with the more obviously biological aspects of our nature – the influence, say, of a particular hormonal secretion to our brain rhythms – it usually makes good sense to attempt a replication. It none the less remains an error, where such replications do not work, to reject the original study out of hand.[10]

9. These tests show how often a given set of results would crop up, if their source were in fact working randomly. Some journals will only accept a result if it reaches the 5 per cent level of significance; that is to say, if it is a result a random number machine would produce on fewer than 1 in 20 occasions. For an introduction to such statistical techniques, see Siegel (1956).
10. Again, we are on delicate ground. It simply is not clear when a study constitutes a formal replication and when it does not. This is because even the most primitive aspects of human activity *may* be influenced by particular combinations of cultural, psychological, biological or physical circumstances. At any of those levels, events may possess an important individuality of configuration that a replication study fails to match.

If we take more obviously psychological attributes as our example, we will see why this is so: the relation, say, of the frequency with which we recall our dreams to the degree of our respect for authority. Let us say that, on 23 September 1973, we establish an interesting-looking connection between these two variables. Using a group of fifteen-year-olds from a suburban school in Tel-Aviv, we find that authoritarian children recall few dreams. What would our replication be? We cannot simply repeat the study, detail by detail, because the children have already undergone the experience once, and will have learnt. If we repeat it on a similar-seeming sample in the same school on 23 September 1974, the cultural context of the children will in all probability have been subject to a small historical shift: in the meantime, there may have been a major war. If we take similar-seeming children in the same year but from a different school, their context at home and school will almost certainly differ in ways we cannot check. If we look at quite different age-groups, or different nationalities, even the semblance of formal replication breaks down.

And so it should; for our assumptions are inappropriate to our subject-matter. If we assume that a result is 'good' only if it generalizes to all people everywhere, we are smuggling into psychology a potent but entirely misleading implication about human nature: that such findings are 'real' only if they manifest themselves irrespective of the social or cultural contexts of the individuals in question. Yet it is his capacity to interact lawfully with his cultural and social settings that makes the human being worth studying in the first place. To require that our results must be universally generalizable is to assume that people are as impermeable as billiard balls; while, on this argument, a form of psychology that allows for an interaction between the biological, social and experiential would be discredited before it began.

By now, the more general moral should be plain. If we allow our analytic assumptions to limit us to what is true of whole populations of people, to people irrespective of their contexts, to what is true about a person in general, or to what he will produce on demand, we will grow old learning little, and deserving to do so. We will end up holding a fistful of propositions that are largely or exclusively banal.

To qualify as genuinely psychological, explanations must deal with the interplay of causes *within the life of an individual*. To test our general interpretations against evidence about groups, in which the interplay within the individual is ignored, is to operate on altogether trickier ground. The collection of such evidence is entirely legitimate, of course; but the inferences it permits are surrounded with more logical pitfalls than we yet know how to circumvent. In this respect, what the philosophers of science tell us about the search for psychological explanations – the formal tramp of hypothesis, deduction and verification (or falsification) – is inadequate. Philosophers, like Karl Popper, who stress the formal properties of scientific explanation are as a consequence less germane (though more readable) than those, like Habermas, who are sensitive to the hermeneutic tradition that draws on literary and historical scholarship, and the search for the best reading that such work continually presents.[11]

The special awkwardness of psychological interpretation is that our concepts are general, but that the focal point of our interpretation remains stubbornly particular: the individual. Sometimes, for the limited purpose of a specific argument, one can get away with evidence about people considered as a sample. But to believe that short-cuts must be possible, and that the individual will evaporate if ignored, is to inhabit cloud-cuckoo-land. It is the collection of statistics about samples that represents the soft option in psychology, not the detailed study of the individual case. And if a good deal of the evidence in the next chapters takes this easy statistical form, this is only to confess, tacitly, that in matters of rigour we still have a long path to tread.

I would like to round off this catalogue of potential confusions with two anecdotes. As a young man, I worked briefly on the admissions ward of a mental hospital, giving psychological tests to new arrivals. Two adolescents, Daphne and Brian, remain vividly in mind. Daphne, a touchingly pretty seventeen-year-old, was unable to do my tests because she was too distraught to concentrate on them. Only later did I discover why. Once a week she was visited by her mother, who stirred her into a state of agonized bewilderment. Thereafter, she gradually recovered –

11. See, for example, Popper (1972), Habermas (1972); also Polanyi (1966), (1973).

in time for next week's visit. Diagnosed as 'schizophrenic' by the hospital's staff, she struck me as not a jot madder than I was. Vulnerable, certainly, but schizophrenic only in as much as that description covers us all from time to time. She stands as a reminder that if she could not concentrate on my tests, hundreds of thousands of others doubtless cannot concentrate either; and for reasons that do no necessary discredit to themselves.

Brian was a sixteen-year-old who reached the hospital calm, but with his head teeming with religious visions. To me, he seemed very mad indeed. The tests I gave him, he did dutifully. He completed an I.Q. test, a word association test, a memory test, and others besides – all with responses as consistent as they were dull. In some desperation I cast about for any device that would record a trace of what I saw before my eyes: a state, if not of 'possession', at least of great strangeness. At last, my hand fell on the Rorschach ink-blot test; a technique I viewed at the time with scepticism. Carefully, as before, Brian settled to his task, pointing out to me the objects that these ink-blots called to his mind. Patiently, he showed me where the shapes were: the first eight images he traced out and identified were all tiny; and each lay in the white paper surrounding the blots, not in the blots themselves. He was seeing shapes I could not see; and at last, after three hours of trying, I had concrete evidence of the gulf that lay between us.

To have pooled or averaged the responses that Brian had given me that afternoon would have been to obliterate the one positive result I had: the only bridgehead between myself and the boy sitting at my side.

4   Some Psychological Concepts

By now I have in all probability dwelt too long on what can go
wrong – though, God knows, the possibilities are by no means
exhausted. And too long, as well, on evidence in isolation from
the ideas around which it is marshalled. So before launching into
a discussion of the mind and its workings, I would like to devote
a few pages to diagrams. Their purpose is to introduce some of
the psychological concepts used in the later chapters, and to
show that, however slippery they may seem in their literary
expression, they none the less possess a latent formality that
simple geometrical models can make clear.

In deploying the particular set of diagrams I have in mind, I
want to begin with the geometrical figure of the octagon. Its
function here is a little like that of an Oriental mandala. It forms
a series of symbolic arrangements that help to spell out the
assumptions that lie buried in the psychological discussion of the
'self'. This function is of course exclusively conceptual. But
such models are not to be sneezed at. They serve the genuinely
heuristic purpose of generating unexpected insights; and, from
the strictly practical point of view, they can be invaluable in
deciding what evidence is worth collecting, and what analyses it
would be wise to attempt.

The octagon is the figure we walk upon in most Victorian
hallways: the eight-sided tile. Set side by side, octagons yield a
mosaic that in some ways resembles the beautiful six-sided pattern of a honeycomb. Conceptually speaking, octagons start to
acquire interesting properties when overlapped. If we draw nine
octagons, overlapping in the way that the diagram in Figure 6
shows, we find, in the middle of the pattern, a structure I shall
call the 'cell'. Like a fortified town, this has an external
boundary, internal subdivisions, and also an *in*ternal boundary.

The cell, in other words, is an angular doughnut: it has space all around it, and a hole in the middle.[1]

This figure helps to objectify a whole vocabulary of psychological ideas that might otherwise strike us as dangerously arbitrary, or even mystical. Consider for example, the following psychoanalytic propositions – drawn in fact from Norman O. Brown's *Love's Body*:

All the boundaries . . . are fortified.

The natural man . . . tries to become an armoured crustacean alert for attack or defense . . .

. . . the external world and inner id are both foreign territory – the same foreign territory.[2]

In Brown's prose, these propositions hover and shift as we look at them. Notice, though, that they are formal properties of our octagonal cell. The cell is 'fortified', both inside and out. On the outside against the alien world of other people: and on the inside against those aspects of our own mental functioning over which we can exert no conscious control. And the 'territories' against which these fortifications are erected flow one into each other – as we see, if we envisage our cell floating, lifebelt-like, on a pond. Our inner world is peopled by symbolic representations of those with whom we cannot cope; and our perception of external realities is influenced in its turn by what our inner world contains.

The idea of fortification is helpful, then; likewise that of the inner and outer 'strangeness'. But the cell has a good deal else to offer. Look again at the diagrams; and especially at the relation of any one cell to its neighbours. These relations are of three sorts. There are neighbours at a distance, with whom no boundary is shared. There are the four much closer cells, with whom an external boundary wall is shared. And, closer still, there are the four that overlap. In this last instance, the external wall of one cell forms part of the *internal* wall of the other. And

1. This approach to solid geometry relates, obliquely, to the work of the American designer Buckminster Fuller. For an introduction, see Critchlow (1969). 'Cells' can be generated three- rather than two-dimensionally; and by using other figures – for example, the triangle, hexagon and, as I shall show in a moment, the circle.
2. Brown (1966), p. 448.

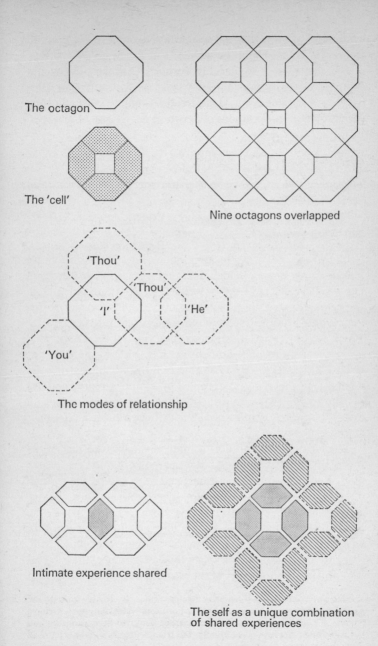

The octagon

The 'cell'

Nine octagons overlapped

'Thou'

'Thou'

'I'

'He'

'You'

The modes of relationship

Intimate experience shared

The self as a unique combination of shared experiences

Figure 6. The symbolic properties of the octagon

vice versa. Our octagons offer, in other words, three degrees of relationship: acquaintanceship, friendship, and intimacy – 'he', 'you' and 'thou'.[3] They also suggest a distinction between friendship and intimacy that we may not have foreseen. The model implies that, in friendship, we use our perception of the other's public 'face' in constructing our own external defences. In an intimate relation, the two concerned are each using the other's public presence in controlling their own irrational desires and fears. To lose a friend is to lose part of one's own public presence; to lose an intimate is to lose part of the bulwark that protects us from our own helplessness.

Nor is this all. Each cell has four segments; and each segment can be construed as a body of experience we share with someone else. Each cell consists, then, of a unique combination of intimate relations.[4] We *are* what we share with those close to us – our parents, our spouses, our children. What is more, we cannot share all of ourselves with any one other person; but only one segment. It follows that, in making sense of our intimate and shared experience, we can only proceed by means of comparison. We can 'triangulate', judging one body of intimate experience in terms of its relation to other such bodies – but total objectivity in such judgments is out of the question. It also follows, because no two people share more than one body of experience, that the two parties to any intimate relationship are bound to see their shared experience in a different light. Unless, that is, theirs is the only intimate relationship they possess – in which case, they suffer a *folie à deux*, and are incapable of making any evaluative judgment about their shared experience at all.

Also, a further refinement, there is an insight into the nature of the strangeness *outside* us. This consists, as we see if we look again at the last of the diagrams, of two elements: (i) the *in*ternal strangeness of those we are intimate with; and (ii) the intimate experience we see them as sharing with others.

More philosophically, there is a delicate point to be made about the way in which each cell is defined. Where in the honey-

3. The philosopher and theologian Martin Buber (1958) suggested that all our relations tend either to be objectifying 'I–It' relationships or intimate 'I–Thou' ones. The octagons offer a refinement on this simple, binary scheme. Farber's (1966) essay on Buber is a most illuminating one.
4. Mary McCarthy's (1943) *The Company She Keeps* is an outstanding expression of this conception in literary form.

comb each six-sided cell is defined entirely by its neighbours, with octagons this is not so. Each cell in the present scheme has sixteen walls; but only twelve of these are defined when octagons are overlapped. Each cell, in other words, must provide four of its sides for itself. Intriguingly, these four walls are the ones that are crucial in our relations with our intimate neighbours. They are the four external walls that help to complete the internal defences of our neighbours. Where the honeycomb pattern might be seen as a metaphor of the individual as the sociologist sees him – as the sum of his external relationships with others – the overlapping octagons provide a model more appropriate to the psychologist. That is to say, one in which the 'creative' activity of each cell is vital to the interdependence and reciprocity that intimately related cells set up between them.

Every model has its drawbacks, naturally – in the case of the octagons, an arbitrary regularity and neatness. They imply, surely wrongly, that all relationships are reciprocal; and they make no allowance for relationships that change with time. The present interpretation can also be faulted as excessively personal: some people, especially as they grow older, draw their sense of identity not from other people, but from bodies of ideas and from institutions.

Some of these deficiencies can be overcome if – as in Figure 7 – we transform the overlapping octagons into overlapping circles.[5] In the manner of Venn diagrams, these circular,

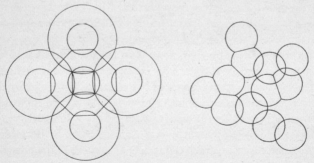

The basic lattices   Overlaps and interfaces
Figure 7. The relation of octagonal to circular cells

5. The octagonal and circular types of lattice are geometrically related, in that octagonal cells result if straight lines are drawn through those points where circular cells intersect.

doughnut-like cells can now be shifted around quite freely in relation to one another; and one of their weaknesses, their lack of interfaces, can partially be overcome by the modification shown in the right half of Figure 7, wherein boundaries are allowed either to overlap, or, in the manner of soap bubbles, to abut.

Another alteration concerns the nature of the boundaries themselves: whether rigidly fixed, like a fortified wall, or permeable, permitting traffic to and fro. This distinction, represented schematically in Figure 8, is of importance psychologic-

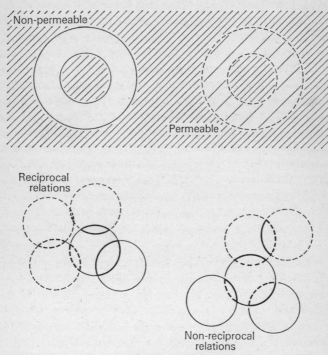

Figure 8. Permeable and non-permeable boundaries

ally speaking, and a good deal depends upon it. For if boundaries are non-permeable, the space they enclose can differ qualitatively from the world outside; whereas if they are in some sense 'porous', the difference between the enclosed and unenclosed becomes more a matter of degree. Using the imagery of sea wall or dike, or that of the bridge-builder's caisson, we may say that the greater the impermeability of the boundary, the 'drier' the enclosed space can be.

Now if the individual does seal himself off in this way from the alien, two consequences follow – one rather obvious, and the other more remarkable. The first is that he will be in a state of constant vigilance, seeing any breach of his boundaries as tantamount to total disaster. Like an astronaut or deep-sea diver, a great deal of his energy will be consumed in boundary maintenance. And secondly, he will feel safe within his defensive arrangements, but also oddly empty, divorced from the turbulence and vitality that he senses in the alien world outside. The more rigid his defences, the emptier he will feel; and the more likely he will be to assume that the unknown embodies the fertility that his own interior life lacks.

It is just this sense of emptiness that one of the most valuable of psychoanalytic insights conveys. For the self is seen as once-alien territory that has been successfully colonized or tamed. This process of capture, whereby the individual takes in elements of the alien and treats them as his own has, however, a most regrettable consequence. Namely that '. . . everything he regards as real he also regards as outside himself; everything he takes "in" immediately becomes unreal and "spectral" '.[6]

And conversely, of course, the more porous an individual's boundaries are to the alien, the more likely he is to place faith in his own emotional workings, and to see them as imbued with some inherent value and meaning.

This theme of the empty or 'unreal' self echoes through much recent writing about human identity. Two formulations have been especially influential: Erving Goffman's stress on the theatricality (and, by implication, falsity) of our social transactions, and R. D. Laing's use of the existential notion of the 'false self'.[7] These ideas clearly draw on the same stock as does that of boundary maintenance. My feeling, though, is that the version offered here avoids the reductive tendency of the others

6. Brown (1966), p. 148. It has recently been argued that Freud himself viewed mental events as unreal; Casey (1972).
7. Goffman (1959), Laing (1960). The existential position – or, at least, an intelligent variant of it – holds that the rational calculations of normal life ensnare us into routines that we perceive as false, and that the expression of the 'true' self is something that we can realize only in action that is unpremeditated.

(Goffman's particularly), and is also the most versatile of the three, applying neatly to bodies of ideas as well as to the people who produce them. It is often said, for example, of the physical sciences that their pasts are 'dead'. Once an aspect of the unknown has been brought fully under control, it ceases to have immediate relevance, and is consigned to the dead space that lies within the discipline's boundary walls. In contrast, paintings, poems, music, and even the thoughts of scholars in disciplines like history, psychology or philosophy, frequently remain vividly alive. To adopt a biological metaphor, they are 'seminal': they retain their capacity to rekindle our imaginative fires.

It is for just this reason that critics of science and technology have sometimes seen the impulse underlying scientific research as pathological. Rather than seeking 'to preserve and enrich life', they claim, science seeks 'to return life to the peace of death'.[8] At a more prosaic level, it is certainly worth noticing that young physical scientists are only rarely taught their discipline by reference to its history, whereas young specialists in the humanities usually are. The presence or absence from the curriculum of the history of psychology is, as a consequence, an excellent index of the ebb and flow of scientistic sentiment through the minds of those planning the instruction.

The idea of the permeability of boundaries also has a bearing on our aesthetic responses – our responses, especially, to works of art. Whilst in the last section of this book I shall assume that some division of our experience into the safe and the alien is inescapable, I shall go on to argue that works of art are symbolic devices that enable us to play boundary games along this frontier – games that allow us to believe that all such necessary distinctions can for the moment be miraculously dissolved.

And last but by no means least, the idea of permeability provides a way of envisaging relationships that change over time, and are non-reciprocal. The lower half of Figure 8 shows four relationships in which the participants are equally poised, at least in relation to each other; and four more in which there is an imbalance. (A solid line in that diagram indicates that its owner

8. Brown (1959), p. 78; also Brown (1966). On this important but, I believe, over-simplified view, 'to be is to be vulnerable'. The function of intellectual control is thus to protect ourselves from the suffering that our own vulnerability entails.

46

is impervious to the other's perception of who they both are; a dotted line that he is receptive to what the other person thinks.) It takes little imagination to see that the doughnut-like cells can now be arranged serially, to describe the shifts that occur in the course of a relationship, with degrees of intimacy, states of emotional openness and patterns of reciprocity altering over time. Figure 9 shows one such sequence: a species of psychological strip cartoon. The story is one you may like to decipher

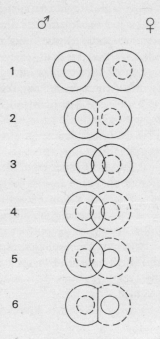

Figure 9. Changes in a relationship over time

for yourself. Notice as you do so, though, that events of cardinal significance occur in the third and fourth frames. Not only does the relationship undergo a 'catastrophic' shift of the kind discussed by Zeeman, but the psychic organization of both partners undergoes an enduring change.[9] The male, on the left, emerges with a pattern of organization initially enjoyed by his female partner; while she, figuratively speaking, is turned inside out. The moral, a potent one, is that for better or worse, relationships

9. Zeeman (1971), Isnard and Zeeman (1974).

frequently transform those who pass through them; that it is usually an intimate relationship that mediates radical psychological change.

The establishment of such sequences suggests, finally, a sophistication of the original idea of the 'cell' – a three-dimensional stack of 'selves', arranged one on top of the other like a layer cake. As with the octagons, we can turn to architecture for an illustration: in this case, to those perspective drawings produced during the late fifteenth and early sixteenth centuries by men like Jan Vredeman de Vries (see Plate 1). In some of the most conspicuously beautiful of these, we look up inside towers – usually, as it happens, octagonal in structure. The towers are segmented, floor by floor, each layer representing a stylistic variation on the common structural theme. Vredeman's drawings do have a powerfully evocative, even mystical property; and it seems only a small distortion of his intention to use these layered towers as a metaphor for the organization of the self – each floor standing for a separate epoch in the developing life of the individual. In such a conception, the person's past coexists with his present as do the various layers in an archaeological excavation, the transition from one to the next demanding of us a distinct shift of tone and style. Occasionally, the discontinuities are all that remain to us of some cataclysm; but more often they represent the evolution, step by step, of a survival strategy in which costs and benefits are balanced against one another in most complex ways. It is to these complexities that I now want to turn.

Part Two

People Themselves

5   The Management of Impulse

Having dwelt at length on psychology and psychologists, it is high time we looked at the ordinary mortals psychologists are supposed to study. Accordingly, this chapter presents two pieces of evidence about people, and it does this in some detail. The first concerns a young boy; the second a number of adults. Each is eloquent in its own right, but they also resonate on one another in an illuminating way. Their purpose is in this sense illustrative. I shall use them to show why psychological boundaries spring into being, and also to say something about their implications for the individuals whose psychic lives they divide up. In doing this, I shall make use of a second interpretative concept: 'the management of impulse'.

The first body of evidence consists of sixteen drawings.[1] These were produced one after the other, within an hour or so, by a boy we shall call Peter, who was then five years old. A tight-knit series, they illustrate the twists and turns of a child's mind in the face of a major emotional threat. They are supplemented by notes that his mother wrote at the time.

Peter is the elder son of upper-middle-class parents. Now in his teens, he shows every sign of being a normal, conventionally well-adapted young man. He has had no contact with the profession of psychotherapy, nor appeared to need it; and is exceptional only in that he comes from a broken home. His parents were divorced when he was three, and thereafter, his contacts with his father were minimal. Peter produced his drawings at a moment in his life when his virtual monopoly of his mother's attention was for the first time unambiguously threatened: on the morning after his new stepfather – whom he already knew well – arrived as a fully-fledged member of the

1. See Plate 2.

household. Although Peter's relations with his stepfather are described in his mother's notes as 'amiable', his stepfather's arrival represented a major incursion into his proprietorial attachment to his mother.

On the morning in question, his mother records, Peter was visibly upset. Lately he had been troubled with nightmares; and, after some prompting, he eventually acknowledged that he had had another. His mother suggested that he make a drawing of it. He did this, and the other fifteen drawings that followed, sitting by himself in the garden, coming indoors frequently to show his handiwork to both adults. It seems that the adults asked Peter only a few questions about the drawings as they were presented, but encouraged him each time to produce another. His mother's notes stress that he worked at first with 'hectic speed', but that, as the series progressed, he became slower and slower.

Apart from the last one, all the sixteen drawings consist of two figures: on the right, the 'aggressor', and on the left, his 'victim'. In the first fifteen drawings, the aggressor wields a knife or sword, and lacerates the victim with it. Although he had drawn such demonic figures in the past, Peter had never previously linked them directly to himself. But his mother's notes are emphatic: he identified the aggressor *both* as the horn-headed, foul-smelling men who had been haunting his dreams, *and* as 'Peter' – himself. The victim was identified, after some prevarication it seems, as his stepfather. And there is no doubt that Peter found the drawings frightening, the first one especially. This should scarcely surprise us, of course: they were the stuff of his nightmares; and the stuff, too, of his feelings about the stepfather to whom the drawings were being shown.

What, then, do the drawings tell us? In each of the first fifteen drawings (Drawing 16 represents a complete change of subject-matter), the 'Peter' figure is cutting the 'Stepfather' figure with an instrument: the Peter figure hands out the punishment, and the Stepfather figure absorbs it. Drawing 1 establishes the theme, and contains certain recurring elements.

The attack is initially (Drawings 1–3) on the head; but then (4–8) moves to the body. It then returns to the head (9–10); goes down once again to the body (11–14); and returns at last to the head (15). To begin with, the wounds to the head are open slashes; but gradually they take on more the form of denser, neater obliterations, the clearest expression of this being in Drawing 10. The attacks to the body are more thrusts: a matter of running Stepfather through.

Next, the weapon. This begins as a knife; but gradually engthens into a sword, sometimes rather indistinctly drawn. By Drawing 10, this indistinctness is gone: the sword is now a neat line – a rapier, perhaps, or even a blackboard pointer.

The two figures also fluctuate in terms of their relative size and coherence. In Drawing 1, the Peter figure is the larger of the two. In Drawings 2–4, the two figures are more nearly equal. In Drawing 5, the Peter figure begins to swell and the Stepfather to shrink; and in Drawing 12, the Peter figure is massively the larger of the two. By this stage, the Stepfather's body has not merely shrunk but floated apart, disintegrated.

Now, look at the Peter figure's face. In Drawing 1 this is clearly articulated: large gaping mouth, upturned at the corner; sharp, separate teeth; large staring eyes; hair with horns. By Drawing 3 the face has become chaotic. The horns disappear by Drawing 6, not to reappear until Drawing 12. The eyes remain reasonably prominent, but they are less penetrative in their gaze. The hair, arguably, lingers until Drawing 6, but thereafter the Peter figure is bald. The expression of the mouth goes through some curious changes too. It becomes very wide-gaping by Drawing 7, but shrinks up again in 11 and 12. In Drawing 11, especially, there are curious lines radiating like huge creases from the mouth that occur nowhere else.

Lastly, the severed entities on the floor. Peter's mother leaves no doubt that these were identified by Peter, after some uneasy giggling, as the Stepfather's 'wee' – his penis.

What are we to say? What interpretation can we offer? It is clear, straight away, that the nature of the attack launched by the Peter figure on the Stepfather figure varies as the sequence proceeds. In Drawing 1, there are both facial slashes and what can retrospectively be construed as castration. By Drawing 10, one sees a different story: the neat obliteration of the Stepfather's features with an instrument that looks precise and ruler-like. The Stepfather's limbs, moreover, have floated away from his body. He is a non-person. Although in Drawing 12 the castration is explicit, the tone is quite unlike that of Drawing 1. In a sense, the series could be said to culminate in Drawing 12. There, the

Peter figure is master: calm and controlled, compared to the vicious glee of Drawing 1, and to the backwash of chaos that the drawing of Peter's face then seems to suggest (Drawings 3, 4 and 6). The Stepfather is no more than a figment; cancelled out, administratively destroyed.

After Drawing 12, too, the series peters out. The conviction of the drawing slackens; and in Drawing 16 the subject-matter changes abruptly, becoming the model ship and aeroplane that Peter and his stepfather had been making the day before. An echo of the aggressive feeling remains – the aeroplane is a bomber; but the format has reverted again to that of playing at war.

The drama is over, in other words. But if we take Drawing 12 – the magisterial castration – as the culmination of the series, there are interpretative snags. In the first place, it was Drawing 1, not Drawing 12, that Peter himself evidently saw as the most potent. Drawing 12 did not correspond to any special peaking of energy or concern on Peter's part; it simply stood relatively late in a series produced with gradually slackening speed and fervour.

Peter's drawings, then, are not simply the *expression* of violent and conflicting impulses towards his stepfather. Rather, they are a device he uses in coming to terms with those impulses: a way of learning to cope with them. Drawing 12 is the point in the series at which the various manœuvres Peter employs against his stepfather coincide: (i) the Peter figure's great size; (ii) his confidence; (iii) his sharp but precise weapon; (iv) the facial slashes; (v) the obliteration of the face; (vi) the disintegration of the stepfather's body; and, last but not least, (vii) his castration. Although all seven of these manœuvres seem to have been useful to Peter, none of them, on the present evidence, seems to be pre-eminent.

These drawings of Peter's are eloquent in ways so obvious that one takes them too much for granted. First, last, and overwhelmingly, they are *symbolic*. In the literal, dictionary definition sense, they are physical signs that 'stand for' experiences that Peter cannot utter in any more direct way. The nightmare figures that haunted Peter can only be seen as symbols; personifications of violent emotions of which Peter was not fully aware. The process whereby these figures were brought out of hiding, into the everyday world of mother and stepfather, garden and kitchen, was itself doubly symbolic. The aggressor stood for creatures Peter had dreamed about. They also formed a tacit communication between Peter, his mother and his stepfather; one that enabled him to articulate to them his feelings of resentment or desperation. And the drawings themselves constitute a symbolic language, in terms of which the manœuvres essential to Peter's management of his violent feelings could occur. They were his fetish, into which he could stick his pins; the Punch and Judy, in terms of which he could move from nightmare rage to masterful control.

Whether or not we accept classically Freudian views about castration and its attendant anxieties, the fact also remains that the detachment of his stepfather's penis is an image that has sprung spontaneously to Peter's mind. His mother remarks in her notes that Peter did not at that time know 'the facts of life'. That is to say, he had no explicit knowledge of the singular part played by his stepfather's penis in his relationship with his – Peter's – mother; nor the part played by penises in all relationships between fathers and mothers, step- or otherwise. None the less, it was an element of his tacit knowledge; part of the knowledge that was simply 'there'.

What Peter is achieving in his drawings is a matter of internal defence or control. But it is not just that. Although he is manœuvring to contain violent impulses, he is also *harnessing* them, turning them to good account. Through his drawings, he is establishing for himself a habitable niche in a situation that would otherwise be uninhabitable.

It is this adaptive use of symbolic devices that we call *management*. And it is through such management of impulse that we create a stance from which we can explore; venturing 'inwards' into the jungly terrain of our own emotions, and 'outwards' towards other people. If we are lucky, we weld together a coherent style of management in which our public selves express our private needs; and in which our needs are in their turn concordant with what we can publicly achieve.

Such a state of grace is one that few of us consistently achieve. For, in the realm of the mind, law and order are usually achieved at an inhuman cost. The rest of the chapter deals with what that cost is.

Peter we saw struggling to find some way of coping with violent emotions that threatened to swamp him. Later in life sadly, he is more likely to find that these processes of management have become all powerful; and that a violent impulse is an experience he can recapture only fleetingly, and in subtly reconstituted forms. The second piece of evidence shows what shape these processes of management can take. This material comes from a notorious experiment conducted by the American psychologist, Stanley Milgram. Again, we see people trying to cope with an unusually stressful situation – though the situation is artificially contrived, and those facing it are adults. But here, in the adult world, the boot of management is on the other foot. It is no longer the impulse that is sovereign; rather the mechanisms of control. As we grow up, the devices we learn to use in colonizing our own emotions themselves take on a dictatorial power.

The publication of Milgram's results in the 1960s created an uproar, and efforts have since been made to outlaw such work as too gross an infringement of the professional decencies. A deeply disquieting study, it is objectionable for the deception it involved. Like war and disaster, it is revealing all the same; and what it tells us about human beings is hard to bear.[2]

Milgram took ordinary adult American volunteers – 'postal clerks, high-school teachers, salesmen, engineers, and labourers' – and invited them to take part in a study of the effects of punishment on simple skills. They were told that, in the interests of science, they were to give electric shocks to an experimental victim every time he made a mistake. Milgram's dupes had before them a 'shock generator' with a voltage scale ranging from 15 to 450 volts. The scale bore eight labels: 'Slight Shock', 'Moderate Shock', 'Strong Shock', 'Very Strong Shock', 'Intense Shock', 'Extreme Intensity Shock', 'Danger: Severe Shock', and simply 'XXX'. The victim was out of sight, but not out of earshot; and the dupe's instructions were to step up the level of shock for every error he made. If the dupe faltered, he was subjected by the experimenter to four verbal prods. These were 'please continue' or 'please go on'; 'the experiment requires that you continue'; 'it is absolutely essential that you

2. Milgram (1970), (1974). These results were first published in 1963.

continue'; and, finally, 'you have no other choice, you *must* go on'.

Milgram's volunteers were of course tricked. There was no electrical shock; and the victim's yells and moans were a pretence. But two important results emerge from this macabre undertaking. The first is that many of the dupes suffered great distress:

In a large number of cases the degree of tension reached extremes that are rarely seen in socio-psychological laboratory studies. Subjects were observed to sweat, tremble, stutter, bite their lips, groan, and dig their finger-nails into their flesh ... Fourteen of the 40 subjects showed definite signs of nervous laughter and smiling. The laughter seemed entirely out of place, even bizarre. Full-blown, uncontrollable seizures were observed for 3 subjects. On one occasion we observed a seizure so violently convulsive that it was necessary to call a halt to the experiment ...[3]

The second result was that, despite this suffering, all Milgram's dupes went on increasing the shocks until they reached levels far beyond any sane expectation. All pressed on until they reached the 'Intense Shock' level, the first to baulk finally doing so at 300 volts. The large majority, however, went beyond this; and well over half went to the very top of the voltage scale: 450 volts labelled 'XXX'.

It is hard to forgive the false objectivity of a phrase like 'Full-blown, uncontrollable seizures were observed for 3 subjects ...', coming from the man who had wilfully induced the seizures in the first place. But more is demanded of us here than mere censoriousness. As Milgram makes plain, we are witness to the processes that enable ordinary citizens, in certain circumstances, to commit acts that they would otherwise view as atrocities. Obedience comes easily and often. It is a ubiquitous and indispensable feature of social life. As Milgram observes, 'Obedience is the psychological mechanism that links individual action to political purpose. It is the dispositional cement that binds men to systems of authority.'

Milgram created a situation in which his victims saw the psychological experimenter as exercising legitimate authority;

3. Milgram (1970), p. 293.

and it is the notion of legitimacy that holds the key. Granted the definition of a situation as legitimate, men will rape, pillage and murder. As the fate of European Jews testifies, they will even operate the grotesque apparatus of genocide, and do so with no more distress than those of Milgram's victims who moved to the 450-volt position, yet remained 'calm throughout', showing only 'minimal signs of tension from beginning to end'.

What is so odd about kindliness and brutality is the *flimsiness* of the excuses we require for switching from one mode to the other; and yet the ease with which we can keep them in water-tight compartments. The man who, in his normal office-going life, moves in trepidation of muggers and is chronically agitated by the spread of urban crime, will – if the situation is appropriately redefined for him as one of 'war' – hose down innocent women and children with napalm, and do so with a conscience that is only a little troubled. The setting becomes one in which ordinary people find themselves free to indulge impulses they did not know they possessed.

The truth must be, then, that adults as a whole are ruled not by naked impulses, sadistic or otherwise, but by the definition of boundaries in terms of which such impulses are controlled – or, from time to time – unleashed. The behaviour of ordinary mortals is governed by their sense of what is normal, legitimate or fitting. In warfare, all the peacetime definitions of normality and legitimacy are altered; and the bank manager, insurance clerk and Sunday School teacher act out the drama of Peter's drawings.

Other equally bizarre dissociations are to be found scattered throughout our society: the ritual of the gynaecological examination, for instance. Every day, throughout the Western world, staid women of all ages allow men they do not know, often accompanied by groups of young students of both sexes, to examine and discuss parts of their body that they normally shelter even from their husbands or lovers – parts of their bodies around which centre the elaborate gradations of self-disclosure and self-expression that go to make up their sense of themselves as women. Yet, if the situation is defined as 'medical', they bare themselves on the instant to the probing hands and by no means entirely impersonal gaze of complete strangers. This staggering transposition, like Milgram's experiment, generates anxiety. What is amazing is that it is possible at all.[4]

To those used to traditional lines of demarcation in academic life, the argument may seem to be in danger of scattering itself: part in the biology of drives and impulses, part in the sociology of cultural definitions, part in the psychology of anxieties and needs. However, the nervous observance of such academic boundaries obscures a coherence in the behaviour of an individual, in which the biological, sociological and psychological facets of his experience interact. As an example of such an interaction, consider the model latent in a book by Jules Henry, *Culture Against Man*.[5]

In *Culture Against Man*, Henry devotes considerable space to a description of 'Rome High', an American high school in a lower-middle-class suburb; and to 'Tight-Pants Teen-Town', a commercial dance-hall where the young of Rome went for their entertainment. If Milgram's study carries an implicit criticism of American adults of the 1950s, Henry's is a blistering critique of the world those adults created for their children. He stresses the extent to which, in the barren rootlessness of their lives, the Rome adolescents come increasingly to depend on the ritual aggression of the football pitch and on the ritual sexuality of the dance-floor.

Henry's argument implies a vicious circle in which there are three elements: (i) a sense of rootlessness, or *anomie*; (ii) the need for the expression of violent and dissociated impulses; and (iii) the commercial exploitation of that need. The circle works very simply. In a state of rootlessness, humans fall back upon the expression of relatively primitive impulses. These may be sexual or aggressive; they may take the form of playing with danger, or of experimenting with drugs. The hallmark of such stimulus-seeking is its dissociated or 'split' quality: it is behaviour that is

4. Emerson (1970). It is sociologists who have concerned themselves, correctly, with 'the definition of the situation': McHugh (1968). Sadly, though, the word 'situation' is itself being rapidly drained of meaning. Together with 'problem' and 'interact', it now forms a deadly triumvirate of jargon – the perfect protection against insight. Such terms are hard to avoid, as this text shows; but each time we use them, we sink deeper into rhetoric, and slip further from the chances of discovery.

5. Henry (1966).

by definition illegitimate – resolutely irresponsible, and sometimes positively satanic. People with such impulsive needs are ripe for commercial exploitation. They pay to watch violent sport, to listen to hell-raising pop music, and to watch sex and violence on film and television, to buy drugs, to get drunk. The world of make-believe this commercial exploitation creates is remote from any life the ordinary person could hope to lead. The gulf between need and fulfilment thus widens; and the sense of *anomie* deepens in its turn. The need for impulsive expression

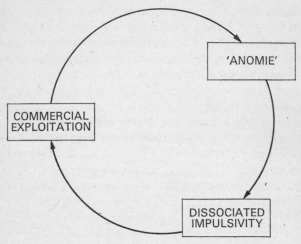

Figure 10. A vicious circle linking the biological, cultural and experiential facets of the individual's life

becomes even more peremptory; and the opportunities for commercial exploitation as a consequence increase. The sense of rootlessness deepens yet again. And so on, in infinite regress.[6] (This vicious circle suggests, incidentally, that if obedience is the disposition that cements men to systems of authority, the link between *anomie* and dissociated impulsivity is what cements commercial exploitation to urban violence.)

This model is almost certainly over-simplified. It will have served its purpose if it establishes that causal patterns are often

6. Marcuse – may the good Lord forgive him his jargon – seems to have an analogous point in mind when he speaks of 'repressive de-sublimation'. Robinson (1969) discusses the 'sexual radicals'; and so does Rycroft (1971).

complex; and that they embrace elements that seem at first sight far-flung.

Lives are embedded in a cultural context; but they take shape in response to urgently experienced needs. It follows that the sociologist's image of human experience as a putty-like substance, pressed by society into one or another cultural mould, is inadequate to our purpose. Likewise, the more traditionally biological conception of human beings, programmed at birth, and rebounding through life as impermeable as billiard balls. However tempting these rival metaphorical systems are, the psychologist must be ready to evolve a language of his own. What is more, neither people nor their cultures are static. Movement from one state to another is frequently painful – but also revealing. The German novelist Hermann Hesse speaks about such transformations and crises in *Steppenwolf*:

Every age, every culture, every custom and tradition has its own character, its own weakness and its own strength, its beauties and cruelties; it accepts certain sufferings as matters of course, puts up patiently with certain evils. Human life is reduced to real suffering, to hell, only when two ages, two cultures and religions overlap . . . there are times when a whole generation is caught in this way between two ages, between two modes of life and thus loses the feelings for itself, for the self-evident, for all morals, for being safe and innocent.[7]

When worlds overlap, there is suffering and a sense of rootlessness. But also, as Hesse goes on to say, there is the possibility of some constructive intervention in events that are otherwise oppressive and predictable. Such conflict occurs within individuals; between one individual and others – Hesse cites Nietzsche as a man born out of his time; and also in societies as a whole. In each case, the consequences reward our close attention. And in each case, it is on the consequences of these conflicts that our evidence should bear.

7. Hesse (1965), p. 28.

6 The Life of the Mind

Evidence like that of Peter's crisis poses some awkward questions. What sort of things are impulses? And how are we to collect evidence about the transformations that the mind performs under their influence? In shaping answers, we hesitate, for the mind is a strange system: there is nothing on earth much like it. The next two chapters marshal some evidence about how it works; and in doing so, they observe two closely related and overlapping principles of organization that the mind is built upon. This chapter deals primarily with the question of *consciousness*: the distinction between those ideas we are aware of, and those we are not. The next chapter predominantly concerns the question of *identity*: the distinction between those desires or actions we acknowledge as our own, and those we reject. Both are aspects of the mind's functioning that help us to stake out the 'familiar', and to separate this from what we consider as 'alien'.

In looking here at the evidence about conscious and unconscious thought, there are three interpretative points to bear in mind. In the first place, far from being a porridge-like and irrational mess, the mental processes of which we are unaware often prove to possess a high degree of *structure*. Indeed, some of the most precise thinking we do seems to be thinking to which we have little access, and over which we exert a minimum of control. Secondly, the distinction between conscious and unconscious is in any case far from clear-cut. There exist massively influential forms of thinking that are strictly speaking neither conscious nor unconscious, but *tacit*. And, thirdly, as Chapter 5 has shown, our thinking is shaped by our *needs*. The legitimacy of these needs, as we perceive them, has a bearing in its turn on the questions of consciousness and identity. For while some thinking is tacit, unconscious or unacknowledged because – it seems – it proceeds most efficiently in that way, other thinking lies beyond the pales of consciousness and identity because we cannot afford to acknowledge that it is taking place.

It is educative to begin by looking at the model of the mind that one of the founding fathers of psychology, Francis Galton, found it helpful to employ. Galton was Charles Darwin's cousin. Nowadays, we tend to see him as a clever man with ugly Victorian prejudices about race and class. (It was he who believed that our intelligence could be measured in the same way as our athletic ability, and he who once said that 'England has certainly got rid of a good deal of refuse through means of emigration'!) Prejudiced he certainly was; and also naïve about 'blood' and human inheritance – he once published a family tree showing that he and Darwin were descended from Charlemagne. On the other hand, he was full of fertile contradictions; and unquestionably he was able to rise from time to time to flights of great ingenuity. He once decided, for instance, that, in the course of a morning walk, he would view everything about him as though he were being spied upon: an idea worthy of the modern American sociologist Garfinkel.[1] By the time he had reached Piccadilly, he tells us, 'Every horse on every cabstand seemed to be watching me either openly or in disguise.' These 'persecutory delusions', entirely self-imposed, lasted for eight or nine hours; and he could easily revive them three months later.[2]

Starting from tests of free association that he performed on himself, he reached a model of the mind not wholly unlike Freud's. It was based on the metaphor of a house:

There seems to be a presence chamber where full consciousness holds court and an antechamber just outside, crowded with ideas lying beyond the ken of consciousness; out of this antechamber the ideas most nearly allied to the problem at issue appear to be summoned in a mechanical or a logical way, and so have their turn of audience.[3]

Beyond or below these two chambers, there was a third, 'a darker basement, a storehouse from which older and remoter ideas can with greater difficulty be called up into consciousness'. Galton goes on to use this model to account for the special competence and originality of those who think well: 'great

1. Garfinkel (1967).
2. Burt (1961).
3. Taken from Burt (1961), p. 15.

orators, men of letters, distinguished scientists'. Their competence springs, he suggests, both from their 'fluency' – the ease with which they recover associations from their mental antechambers; and from the efficiency of the mechanism whereby these ideas – the *appropriate* ideas – are selected for conscious scrutiny. The original, Galton saw as having high fluency and excellent powers of selection. The unoriginal, as good at selecting but lacking fluency. And the mentally unstable, as the victims of the reverse pattern – high fluency but poor selection.

Though neat, this formula is too simple, as we shall see. For Galton sometimes writes as if consciousness and rationality were one and the same.[4] We know, though, that matters are not that easy. All that occurs within the presence chamber is not orderly and rational (we are aware, for instance, of our dreams). And all that takes place outside it, in antechamber and basement, is by no means disorganized or shapeless. Indeed the assumption of unconscious rationality is built into his model by Galton, whether or not he realized this, in the form of the mechanism whereby unconscious ideas are selected for our conscious inspection.

Some of the most elegant evidence of the mind's ability to think while its owner is unawares, is that of 'unconscious work'. Scientists and mathematicians often struggle ineffectively with a problem; lay it aside; and then find the solution coming to them – Eureka! – in the bath, or as they step on to a bus, or in a dream.[5] At a pedestrian level, we have all experienced this in trying to recall a name. We search for it; have it on the tip of our tongue; lose it; give up; and then find, sometimes, that it leaps into our minds, not as a clue or approximation, but complete.

Some instances of 'unconscious work' have been documented with care. One of the most compelling is that of the German poet Rainer Maria Rilke, and the circumstances in which he found himself writing his masterpiece, the fifty-five *Sonnets to*

4. Freud, too, exalted our rationality. He once said that 'the ideal condition of things would of course be a community of men who had subordinated their instinctual life to the dictatorship of reason'. Roazen (1975), p. 161. Freud saw the influence of the unconscious as essentially disruptive; and it was left to his rivals – notably Jung – to grasp something of its constructive function.

5. Hadamard (1945) gives some excellent examples.

Orpheus.[6] These, one of the greatest poetic utterances in any tongue, he wrote, together with a substantial part of his *Duino Elegies*, in a period of nineteen days, between 2 February and 20 February 1922: 1,230 lines of finished verse in all. He claimed that he worked largely without revision, as if 'taking dictation'; and the state of his manuscripts seems to bear this out. This staggering burst of productivity is notable for the effortlessness with which these highly wrought poems found their way, via Rilke's pen, on to the page; and for the surprise they caused their mediator, the poet himself. After years of uneasy inactivity during and after the First World War, Rilke settled himself on 2 February 1922, to write the remaining *Elegies*, completing a task begun as early as 1911. Yet what he in fact wrote were the first of the *Sonnets*, material he knew nothing about, and had no intention of writing down. These first twenty-six *Sonnets*, more than 350 lines of verse, were set down in four days, 'without one word's being in doubt or requiring to be altered'. The experience was one that Rilke describes, in a letter to a friend, as 'perhaps the most mysterious, most enigmatic, dictation I have ever endured and performed'.

He was set free to write, it seems, by the coincidence of two events: the sight in a shop window of an engraving of Orpheus with his lyre; and an account by a woman friend of the death of her adolescent daughter – a girl, Wera Knoop, whom Rilke had met only once or twice when she was a child. Remarkably graceful, Wera was struck down in early adolescence by a mysterious glandular disease. This made her body 'strangely massive', and quite rapidly killed her. The photograph that remains suggests that, before this ailment gripped her, she was ravishingly beautiful (see Plate 3).

In some sense or other, Rilke's *Sonnets* must have 'existed' in his mind, at least as a potential for action, before he found that he had written them down. Twist and turn though we may, short of impugning Rilke's testimony, we cannot avoid the conclusion that highly complex patterns of meaning had taken shape in his imagination without his knowing. These focused on the symbols of Orpheus and the doomed Wera Knoop; and fell out

6. This account is drawn from Leishman's (1949) introduction to the *Sonnets*. These are discussed more autobiographically in Hudson (1972).

into patterns of words, arranged in sonnet form, as the un-suspecting poet began to write.

Where Galton saw logical properties vested in the mechanism that fishes ideas out of the antechamber's associative stream, Rilke's poems are evidence for a stream that is not a stream at all; rather, a somewhat computer-like store which defines the shape and content of conscious thought that has not occurred – and may never do so. In a case like Rilke's, their owner has little conscious say in the form their expression takes. He may edit, prune and supplement, after the event. But, at the time, he is little more than a sluice-gate: an aperture that the flood of meticulously precise, and balanced ideas gushes through.

What is more, we solve problems, paint pictures, write poems according to certain regularities. Ideas – the *right* ideas – typic-ally come to us when we do not expect them. The act of intense concentration seems to create insights and, at the same time, to block the movement of these insights out of the antechamber and into the light of consciousness. In coping with this quirk of the mind's functioning, we learn to be especially alert to our-selves at certain times: moments of transition from one mental state to another, when we are dropping off to sleep, or waking up, or beginning to relax after a period of strain.

Another way of subverting the oppressive effects of our conscious rationality lies in our dreams. An excellent (if hack-neyed) example is that of the German nineteenth-century chemist, Kekulé, and his discovery of the benzine ring:

. . . but it [writing a textbook] did not go well; my spirit was with other things. I turned the chair to the fireplace and sank into a half sleep. The atoms flitted before my eyes. Long rows, variously, more closely united; all in movement wriggling and turning like snakes. And see, what was that? One of the snakes seized its own tail and the image whirled scornfully before my eyes. As though from a flash of lightning I awoke; I occupied the rest of the night in working out the conse-quences of the hypothesis . . . Let us learn to dream, gentlemen.[7]

This discovery of Kekulé's holds two morals for us: one obvious, the other not. The first is that Kekule was a tough-minded physical scientist who found the solution to a technical problem in a territory that scientifically minded psychologists, themselves eager to be like physical scientists, urge us to ignore.

7. See Hudson (1973b).

The second moral is more awkward to state, but we should attempt it. For Kekulé is not the first man in history to have dreamt about snakes; creatures that writhe their way through the mythology of most cultures, and crop up in fantasies of many of those cultures' inhabitants. The snake that swallows its own tail is known to us, for example, from the classical myths of the Greeks. The possibility must exist, therefore, that Kekulé's dream was drawn not from his own personal experience of snakes, but from a basement stockpile that most of us hold in common. This idea of a stockpile, a 'collective unconscious', creates more distrust than any other in the psychoanalytic canon; perhaps because it was given a mystic and, to most of us, incredible twist by Freud's contemporary Jung. There is no reason, on the other hand, why it should not be discussed in terms that are matter of fact. The unconscious may prove not a 'closet full of skeletons in the private house of the individual mind', but a 'general possession of all mankind'. And it may be so because the contents of our basements are built up symbolically from experiences that most human beings share.

A man much preoccupied with such matters was Giambattista Vico, the eighteenth-century Italian philosopher. He was particularly interested in the assumptions and myths that all members of a given society accept. These spring, he claimed, from the exercise of 'common sense'; that is to say, from 'judgment without reflection'. These myths, the stuff of tacit judgment, envelop us today just as comprehensively as they did in Vico's day. They govern the responses we make automatically, without rational intervention. In everyday language, they are 'instinctive'.[8]

There exists simple paper-and-pencil techniques – Osgood's *semantic differential*, and Kelly's *repertory grid* – that enable us to measure these assumptions.[9] We can ask, for example, whether scientists are 'warm' or 'cold'; whether nurses are 'rough' or 'smooth'. And the regularities we achieve in this way are often little short of astounding. All over the civilized world, people will agree that scientists are cold, hard and manly, and that artists are warm, soft and feminine; irrespective of whether they

8. Bergin and Fisch (1968).
9. Osgood *et al.* (1957), Kelly (1955), Bannister and Fransella (1971).

know anything at first-hand about the arts and sciences or not.[10]

A short exposure to the results of work on such assumptions rapidly convinces you that much of what passes for rational debate is no more than the application to a particular issue of simple frameworks of judgment or 'schemata': dimensions of meaning that are anchored in evidence about the world and its workings only very loosely indeed. For it seems that we are doomed every second to receive more information than any system – human or otherwise – could possibly react to. To cope with what would otherwise be an inundating flood, we are bound to *select*; and, in selecting, any yardstick is better than none.

Our capacity for intuitive, over-simplified judgment is, then, basic to our survival. There exists an important tradition of psychologists, on both sides of the Atlantic, who have used this concept of the interpretative framework or 'schema'. The term 'schema' is one we associate primarily with Frederic Bartlett's studies of remembering; but adaptations of it have been used by George Miller in his discussion of 'plans', and Richard Gregory in talking about the 'hypotheses' the brain uses in coping with the flood of information reaching it from the retina of the eye.[11]

We schematize, then, as automatically as we breathe. But to acknowledge this is only to face ourselves with a further problem: the question, namely, of whether the schemes we use are the 'right' ones. At the level of the functioning of the eye, they are bound to be approximately so, otherwise we would walk into walls. But at that of social judgment, far greater degrees of slippage between schemata and actuality are only too easy to achieve. Our assumptions can be grossly over-simplified, and they can also embody lines of demarcation that are arbitrary.

If you ask roomfuls of students to make judgments about the two typical figures 'scientist' and 'artist', their reactions will reveal a massive dissociation between ideas of personal attractiveness (warm, exciting, imaginative), and ideas of value (intelligent, dependable, valuable). Figures ranked high in attractiveness, like the 'novelist', 'poet' and 'artist', are ranked conspicuously poorly in terms of their value. Vice versa, figures

10. Hudson (1968).
11. Bartlett (1932), Miller *et al.* (1960), Gregory (1966). A review of the Bartlettian tradition is given by Zangwill (1972).

like the 'physicist', 'mathematician', 'engineer' and 'research scientist', all high in their ranked value, are judged low in attractiveness.[12]

These clusterings reflect a schism: the belief – itself irrational – that the rational and the sensuous are necessarily cut off from one another and are mutually remote. Such dissociations are part of the 'deep structure' of what our formal education in the arts and sciences transmits. The terms of this polarity are those already familiar from Peter's drawings and Milgram's dupes. Expressed as aspects of Vico's 'common sense', they are the ideas of impulse – in this case, pleasurable impulse – and of righteous control. And it is here that radical critics of our society strike hardest. If schoolchildren think in this way, they may do so because society as a whole observes a dissociation between the machinery of impersonal technology and the more personal aspects of our experience. Here, as elsewhere, our discussion of the structure of the mind flows in and out of a further discussion: that about the structure of the social system in which the individual's experience takes shape – about what that structure is, and what it ought to be.

Perhaps the greatest strength of this radical attack – one thinks of Herbert Marcuse's *Eros and Civilisation*, Norman O. Brown's *Life against Death* – is in its acknowledgment that the roots of rationality are not themselves rational, but more a matter of intuitive commitment, of *passion*.[13] In the absence of this commitment, thinking is just a gymnastic routine we perform with more or less agility; but it can become a way of life into which we pour our energies in a greedy, all-devouring way. A passion, moreover, that can cut us off from the human contact and human reference most of us stubbornly continue to need. Consequently, impersonal rationality, the world of dissociated intelligence and irresponsible ingenuity, emerges from the pages of a book like Norman Brown's as a Frankenstein.

Total commitment to the world of ideas is frequently linked not just to a restriction of personal relationships, but to every appearance of a positive flight from them. Lord Keynes's

12. The full details are given in Hudson (1968).
13. Marcuse (1955), Brown (1959). Brown's is, in my judgment, categorically the better book of the two.

biographical essay suggests that Isaac Newton was a case in point:

Newton was not the first of the age of reason. He was the last of the magicians, the last of the Babylonians and Sumerians . . . His deepest instincts were occult, esoteric, semantic – with profound shrinking from the world, a paralyzing fear of exposing his thoughts, his beliefs, his discoveries in all nakedness to the inspection and criticism of the world . . . Like all his type he was wholly aloof from women. He parted with and published nothing except under the extreme pressure of friends. Until the second phase of his life, he was a wrapt, consecrated solitary, pursuing his studies by intense introspection with a mental endurance perhaps never equalled.

Anyone who has ever attempted pure scientific or philosophical thought knows how one can hold a problem momentarily in one's mind and apply all one's powers of concentration to piercing through it, and how it will dissolve and escape and you find that what you are surveying is a blank. I believe that Newton could hold a problem in his mind for hours and days and weeks until it surrendered to him its secret. Then being a supreme mathematical technician he could dress it up, how you will, for purposes of exposition, but it was his intuition which was pre-eminently extraordinary . . .[14]

Until after his mental breakdown at least, Newton seems to have exemplified the way of life we know as the 'flight into work'. Such clinical evidence as we possess suggests that this pattern is a flight from tenderness; a shying away from the pleasures of being cosseted and fed. Whatever its cause, Newton's commitment to his work was beautifully adapted to the demands of science. There exist, though, many instances of mental energies being channelled in ways that are more nearly arbitrary.

Two of the most vivid come from studies of people who are in some sense defective. The first concern *idiots savants*; for the most part defective, but who show great skill in certain respects – usually in music, arithmetic, or drawings. Anastasi cites an American survey conducted in the 1930s that found thirty-three such people.[15] Among them was a 27-year-old man, with the mental attributes of a three-year-old. As a small child, he would scribble figures on the bathroom tiles whenever he could get hold of a pencil. However, he never learnt to talk; achieved nothing at school; and was admitted to an institution at the age of sixteen. Although his hearing was normal, he could not carry on a

14. Keynes (1951), p. 311. See also McGuire and Rattansi (1966), and Storr (1972).
15. Anastasi (1958).

conversation. None the less, he grasped mathematical problems, when they were written down for him, with extraordinary speed. If the figures 2, 4 and 16 were written in a vertical column for him, he immediately continued this, the sixth number being 4,294,967,296. When 9–3 was written, in an attempt to indicate the square root, and when further numbers were written beneath this – 625, 729, and 900 – he produced the square root of each, correctly and at once. Multiplication of several digits by several other digits, he did entirely in his head, writing down only the answer. His skill in this respect had developed, you sense, precisely because other forms of self-expression were blocked.

Even more remarkable is the report of the Russian psychologist Luria about a professional memory man or mnemonist.[16] In this case, the individual's special skill is set against a disability that is harder to pin down. A somewhat rootless individual, he had drifted from job to job, entering music school, becoming a vaudeville actor, then an efficiency expert, and had failed in all these. It was only at this point that he became a mnemonist. Luria says that he had 'a fine wife and a son who was a success'; but that he perceived them, as he perceived all life, 'through a haze'. He lived in a world of hallucinatory visual images, and these he used as the basis for his powers of recall. In his book *The Mind of a Mnemonist*, Luria gives a detailed account of how this extraordinary man's mind worked. On one occasion he listened to several stanzas of Dante's *Divine Comedy* in Italian, a language he did not know. He could reproduce these perfectly, as long as they were read to him distinctly, with slight pauses between the words; and he could do this without warning, *fifteen* years later. Likewise, with an elaborate and meaningless mathematical formula.

His technique was in each case breathtakingly cumbersome. The first line of the *Divine Comedy* runs as follows:

Nel mezzo del cammin di nostra vita . . .

Luria's mnemonist worked as follows:

(Nel) – I was paying my membership dues when there, in the corridor, I caught sight of the ballerina Nel'skaya.
(mezzo) – I myself am a violinist; what I do is to set up an image of a man, together with (Russian: vmeste) Nel'skaya, who is playing the violin.

16. Luria (1969).

(del) – There's a pack of Deli Cigarettes near them.
(cammin) – I set up an image of a fireplace (Russian: kamin) close by.
(di) – Then I see a hand pointing toward a door (Russian: dver).[17]

And so on and on, line after line of poetry that he did not in the least understand. In addition, he could use visual imagery to influence the temperatures of his left and right hands; increasing the skin temperature of his right hand by imagining that he had put it on a hot stove, and then lowering that of his left, by picturing himself holding in it a piece of ice. He could produce 'a distinct depression' of the electrical activity of his brain by imagining that a bright light was flashing in his eyes; and an analogous reaction in his inner ear by imagining a piercing sound.[18]

Luria goes on to show that while this system of visual imagery was almost magically effective, it had drawbacks. His memory man could not take shortcuts; and, more important, he could not forget his images once established. He was haunted by the contents of his own memory store: a hopelessly overburdened remembering machine.

In attempting to make sense of the *idiots savants* and the memory man, the tug of hydraulic imagery is, I find, irresistible. Overwhelmingly, you have the sense of a flow of energy, like water in an irrigation system, blocked at most of its normal outlets and building up a quite exceptional pressure in those few that are open. The consequence is a degree of skill that is out of keeping with the performance that more normally endowed people could muster. This interpretation suggests that the intellectual skills normal people display are limited, in practice, not so much by innate restrictions to their various 'channel capacities', as by the amount of motivating energy they are able to bring to bear on the tasks in question. It is the need to think that fuels the conceptual elaboration; while, conversely, the level of skill reached evidences the strength of the need that underlies it.[19] This train of thought leads us to expect that limits in

17. Luria (1969), p. 45.
18. Such accomplishments may be more widespread than we realize.
19. Both the shape of our various 'channels' and the strength and variability of our needs may be subject to genetic as well as to environmental influence. The topic of inherited differences between individuals (and races) is at the moment, however, in a state of profound muddle – as I shall try to show in Chapter 11.

channel capacity are rarely reached; and that many individuals' levels of accomplishment will alter dramatically, for better or worse, as their emotional states alter – when they move as children from one teacher to another, or undergo domestic crises, or move as young adults from college, where they are working for someone in authority, to, say, research, where they are working for themselves.

More generally, the evidence about *idiots savants* and the memory man encourages us to ask questions about the nature of the cortical damage they have presumably suffered – a territory touched on in Chapter 8. Taken with the other evidence offered here, it also edges us towards questions about the nature of consciousness that are altogether harder to pose. For if skills can develop in this way, as isolated and potentially tyrannous elements of our mental architecture, and if skills can flourish, in any case, with little conscious intervention, we are led to wonder why we are conscious at all. To put the matter quite crudely, why are we endowed with presence chambers in the first place?[20]

I confess I have no idea whether this is a sensible question or not. My own inclination is to concentrate on those aspects of the problem that clearly are practical. Namely, the question of the placing, in each individual, of the boundary between what he is conscious of and what he is not, and the consequences of altering this placing on the way in which he thinks. The more hazardously speculative aspects of consciousness are worth bearing in mind, even so, as a reminder that in psychological research deep (and perhaps bottomless) conceptual pits are rarely far away.

20. Questions of this sort hover, too, around research that attempts to simulate human intelligence with computers.

7 Of Men and Masks

Adjacent to the question of consciousness is that of identity: the sense that each of us possesses of who he is, and what thoughts we can properly acknowledge as our own. Conceptually, the terrain is trying, for ideas like 'identity' and 'self' are by no means easy to handle. There exists, none the less, several pertinent bodies of evidence. These concern such issues as the use of drugs; the states of hypnosis, dissociation and possession; and the experimental study of role-playing. Running through this material, and unifying it, is the concept of the boundary: our capacity to erect 'walls' that separate who we are from who we are not. And, within those defining boundaries, to construct subdivisions that partition each of us into discrete segments or chunks.

Some of the most vivid demonstrations of boundary states come from studies employing drugs. The field of psychopharmacology, though, is large; and one piece of evidence must stand for the rest.[1] This is Oliver Sacks' recent study of the drug L-Dopa and its effect on those suffering from sleeping sickness.[2] Between 1916 and 1927, the world experienced an epidemic of *encephalitis lethargica*, a disease that sprang up with mysterious suddenness and disappeared likewise, having, in Sacks' phrase, taken or ravaged the lives of more than five million in the process. A third of those affected died in coma, or in states of sleeplessness 'so intense as to preclude sedation'. Some survivors were left totally inert, like 'extinct volcanoes'; and remained in that state for as long as fifty years. Others underwent periodic crises, in which they were wracked by a great diversity of violent and conflicting impulses; but, gradually, they too lapsed into immobility.

1. Joyce (1971) offers an introduction to this field.
2. Sacks (1972), (1973).

Such patients were packed away into mental hospitals and special colonies and forgotten. Sacks describes the effects on a few survivors of a drug, L-Dopa, that had proved of some value in the treatment of a quite separate ailment, Parkinson's Disease. The effect was quite abrupt:

One patient, who had been totally transfixed physically and mentally for over thirty years, intensely rigid, completely motionless and mute, showed no reaction whatever as the dose was built up, and then suddenly – in the space of five seconds or less – 'awoke', jumped to her feet, ran down the corridor, and burst into voluble conversation with the dumbfounded nursing staff on her ward. One could not witness such 'awakenings' without feeling their legendary and fantastic quality . . . The first awakenings nearly always gave intense and unmixed joy . . .

. . . one patient . . . burst, on 'awakening', into a flood of anecdotes and allusions all relating to 1926, her last year of real feeling, before her pathological sleep closed around her . . . She said that she knew perfectly well it was 1969 and she was 64, but that she felt as if it was 1926 and she was 21, and that she couldn't imagine what it was like being older than 21.[3]

Whether through the chemical effects of L-Dopa, or through the incompatibility of who they felt they were with who they knew they had become, the outcome for Sacks' patients was distressingly poor. Sacks remarks on the diversity of his patients' subsequent crises, but mentions certain broad categories. One of these he calls 'kinematic':

Patients who are walking or talking normally are suddenly cut off without the slightest warning, stopped in mid-stride, mid-speech and mid-thought; they may stay utterly still for seconds or minutes or hours, as if the ontological film has jammed in one frame; and then, as suddenly, they will be released, and resume their interrupted speaking or thinking, sometimes at the precise point where they left it. These states have no subjective duration whatever . . .[4]

There is a great deal that is startling about these men and women; not least that they could run and speak after thirty years in which they had been physically transfixed. Such work, like Milgram's, is open to objection on humanitarian grounds, the intervention of science having afforded us insight at the expense of suffering to people powerless to protect themselves. But if Sacks' observations are approximately accurate, his patients are

3. Sacks (1972), pp. 522, 523.
4. ibid., p. 523.

an excellent instance of 'catastrophic' change: of the flip-flop alterations of state that occur as we cross a brink. They are evidence, as he points out, for the view that human thought is 'organized and determined as a whole, in its total simultaneous complexity, from moment to moment'.

In retrospect, much of the research published in the 1960s on psychedelic drugs seems, in comparison with Sacks', limply mystical. Suitably dosed – the message was – we become more fully ourselves. The appeal of writings like Timothy Leary's trails off all too easily into a search for 'kicks': an expression of permissive naughtiness, redolent of Jules Henry's vicious circle and the need of the alienated for dissociated thrills.

In many ways more revealing is the phenomenon that fascinated both William James and Freud: hypnosis. For it was Charcot's experiments with hypnosis that launched Freud, then a moderately successful neurologist, on his path of discovery.[5] Strenuous efforts have since been made by the psychological profession to make hypnosis a taboo area, as in some ill-defined way fraudulent. In support of this campaign of persuasion, it is pointed out that if you ask volunteers to impersonate the hypnotic state, their behaviour is often indistinguishable from that of people 'genuinely' hypnotized.[6] Valuable in itself, this evidence has been used to dampen our curiosity about genuine hypnosis and its related states; and this is a shame, because they are, after all, remarkable.[7]

Anthropological, historical and contemporary social evidence combine to convince us that, under certain special conditions, people can undergo physical mutilation without experiencing pain; others will behave as though possessed by spirits; others will remember what they have forgotten, and forget what we would normally expect them to remember. It should not surprise us that such phenomena attract charlatans; but there is no reason why they should not attract psychologists too.

When someone allows a hypnotist to put him into a hypnotic trance, the relationship is one of special trust; and it seems that this trust enables him to achieve kinds of control over his

5. His earlier efforts had included an ill-fated clinical study of cocaine.
6. Orne (1959), Barber (1969).
7. Hilgard (1968), Tart (1969), Fromm and Shor (1972).

physical and mental capabilities that he could not otherwise command. Hypnosis, the evidence suggests, is not a species of sleep, but a species of dissociation: a state in which we are willing to suspend our watchful, integrative monitoring of ourselves, and allow aspects of our experience to go forward separately. Under hypnosis we become highly co-operative; free to play the roles that the person we trust suggests to us.

Such dissociation covers, besides hypnosis, some of the most spectacular of human accomplishments. When St Teresa was possessed by Christ, when a Haitian woman is possessed by voodoo spirits, when conventional citizens undergo religious conversion, something of special psychological interest is taking place.[8] The individual enters into a relation, both trusting and ecstatic, with someone who, materially, does not exist.

More concrete are the effects concerning the sensation of pain:

One of the most striking examples of the impact of cultural values on pain is the hook-hanging ritual still in practice in parts of India ... The role of the chosen man (or 'celebrant') is to bless the children and crops in a series of neighbouring villages during a particular period of the year. What is remarkable about the ritual is that steel hooks, which are attached by strong ropes to the top of a special cart, are shoved under his skin and muscles on both sides of the back. The cart is then moved from village to village. Usually the man hangs on to the ropes as the cart is moved about. But at the climax of the ceremony in each village, he swings free, hanging only from the hooks embedded in his back, to bless the children and crops. Astonishingly, there is no evidence that the man is in pain during the ritual; rather, he appears to be in a 'state of exaltation'. When the hooks are later removed, the wounds heal rapidly without any medical treatment other than the application of wood-ash. Two weeks later the marks on his back are scarcely visible.[9]

More relevant perhaps to members of twentieth-century industrialized society, not given to hook-hanging, is evidence about childbirth: among the more excruciating pains that someone in our own culture can undergo. Yet, as Melzack points out, anthropologists have observed cultures throughout the world which practise a couvade, in which the women show virtually no distress during childbirth:

In some of these cultures a woman who is going to give birth continues to work in the fields until the child is just about to be born. Her husband then gets into bed and groans as though he were in great pain

8. Lewis (1971).
9. Melzack (1973), p. 24.

while she bears the child. In more extreme cases, the husband stays in bed with the baby to recover from the terrible ordeal, and the mother almost immediately returns to attend to the crops.[10]

It would be preposterous to imply that women of our own culture imagine the pain they experience in childbirth. The pain is only too real; but, so too is the fear of childbirth that is an integral part of their upbringing. Fear, muscular tension and a sense of helplessness then become a self-perpetuating cycle; one from which few can break entirely clear.

As notable in their way as hypnosis are the varieties of dissociative mental disturbance that psychiatric textbooks call 'hysterical': blindness, or losses of sensation; sleep-walking and fugue; and also multiple personality. A commonplace in Freud's day, such ailments are on the decline, perhaps because we now no longer assume that our illnesses must take an obviously physical form. The hysteric remains, nevertheless, an identifiable personality type; and the ailments he displays bear a family resemblance to other dissociative conditions like sleep-walking – something, it has been estimated, that some 5 per cent of ordinary, intelligent young men and women do from time to time. Allied but rarer are fugue states. In these, a person will wander from home, disappearing for days, or even years. When, eventually, he 'comes to', he will have little or no idea of where he is, or how he got there. Rarer still are instances of multiple personality, in which two or more separate 'people' may appear to inhabit one body, one central nervous system. These are among our culture's most startling artefacts; there exist barely a hundred recorded cases in all. And hardly ever have they occurred close to psychiatrists sufficiently gifted to describe them.

Despite their rarity, these cases are of riveting interest, because they carry normal properties of mental organization to extreme. Most people experience reversals of mood – not gradual but sharp or catastrophic. And many people also have the sense that they are, in some way, not one person but several. When Angus Wilson speaks of a character falling apart 'into all the various unrelated persons' that 'bobbed up and sank down like corks in the ocean inside', most of us recognize, intuitively, what he is talking about.[11] Likewise with Hesse's *Steppenwolf*,

10. ibid., p. 22.
11. Wilson (1967), p. 382.

who sees himself as a creature divided between man and 'wolf': between responses that are tamed and civilized, and those which are savage.[12]

The first case of multiple personality – of Jekyll and Hyde – to be documented with care was Morton Prince's case of Miss Beauchamp; the best publicized in recent years has been Thigpen and Cleckley's *Three Faces of Eve*.[13] Thigpen and Cleckley's patient, or 'patients', reveal the processes of 'splitting' as clearly as any; and do so in ways that point to the importance of a tension between desire and guilt.

Eve White – the first of Eve's faces – was an anxious young married woman, with a four-year-old daughter. She suffered from marital difficulties, headaches and blackouts. Eve Black – the second face – was the person this married woman turned into when the strain on her became intolerable. Eve Black was as easy-going and irresponsible as Eve White was inhibited and constrained.

This second Eve had existed from childhood. She knew about Eve White; but Eve White knew nothing about her. In the course of Thigpen and Cleckley's therapeutic endeavours, a third face emerged: Jane. A new creation, she knew about both Eve Black and Eve White; but could 'replace' only Eve White. The therapists welcomed Jane as the most responsible, original and sensitive personality of the three, and hoped that she would take over, more and more, the life of the body those three un-easily shared. Just as plausible, however, is the view that Jane took shape in response to her therapists' expectations: a con-summate actress's attempt to please.[14] There is more generally a sense of interpretative self-indulgence about Thigpen and Cleckley's portrayal. It is as if they have decided in advance that three separate personalities co-existed in their patient, and then overlooked all the details crucial to a simpler view. How, for example, did Eve White cope with the presence of Eve Black's clothes in her wardrobe – or, more likely, scattered around her

12. This bifurcation is, as Hesse (1965) says, an 'artless simplification': lives oscillate not merely between two poles but between thousands. Yet the dis-tinction between civilized and savage, 'cooked' and 'raw', remains a pro-foundly influential aspect of our tacit judgment – as the study of stereotyped images in Chapter 6 showed.

13. Thigpen and Cleckley (1957).

14. Osgood and Luria (1954).

bedroom? And her make-up? What did her husband say about her transformations? It is a far more delicate matter than they imply: how are we to distinguish different 'people' from the sharply demarcated moods of a single person?

Cases of multiple personality are very odd; but only, I suspect, because the lines of fissure between the segments of the person in question are so sharply drawn. The two Eves and Jane are *roles*; and they cry out for the metaphorical language of the theatre. But before examining this, we should look at a small experiment that I conducted some years ago. This was based on the Uses of Objects test: a list of everyday items.[15] The test invites you, quite simply, to note down as many uses for each object as you care to. I gave this test three times, in various forms, to a group of seventy young men, aged from fifteen to seventeen. On the first occasion, I offered them the test in the conventional way. On the second and third occasions, four months later, I asked them to do an alternative version of the test, but this time as though they were someone other than themselves. First, as 'Robert Higgins, a successful computer engineer', and then as 'John McMice, the well-known artist'. Higgins was established as a dedicated, conscientious man, with a logical mind and a gift with gadgets. Shy but friendly, he hated woolly ideas and any show of emotion. McMice, in contrast, was established as an un-inhibited, Bohemian figure, who had a taste for coarse and grue-some jokes, and who often said things to shock people. The boys were asked to put their names on the top of their answer sheets, but the confidentiality of what they had written was assured.

Each boy completed the Uses of Objects test three times over: once as himself, once as Higgins and once as McMice. Not surprisingly, Higgins's uses emphasized practical ingenuity, while McMice's were more flamboyant. This was only to be expected. More to the point was the discovery that the very act of playing these two roles seemed to free the boys' minds. Suggestions which were humorous, ingenious, violent or even in the purely statistical sense unusual, were nearly twice as frequent as when the boys had answered in their own right. The increase was one of 93 per cent.

Even more remarkable was the staggering violence and obscen-

15. Hudson (1968) fully describes the study.

ity of some of the suggestions made. Some boys were liberated to a quite alarming degree. Answering as himself, the most violent suggestions one fifteen-year-old mathematics specialist made were:

SHOE: use shoe to knock-out and laces to strangle . . .
SUITCASE: suffocate animals . . .

As McMice he had the following to propose:

MILK BOTTLE: Masturbate with it. Cut my mother's neck with a broken bit. Would have an interesting effect if broken up and shot in little bits at a nude. The milk would be good to drown someone in. Pump it up someone's nose, vagina. Could make a pattern of interesting scars on a little boy's arse. Soak some caviare with it and spoil the dinner.

ONE POUND NOTE: Could buy hormone cream, contraceptives. Give someone a burn on a huge pile of pound notes. Burn it in front of a beggar. Put up vagina, mouth, nose, and burn. Forge it.

CAR TYRE: Run over somebody with it and squash their intestines, genitals, faces. Watch it slimily crush them. Then the car would skid. Fill it with lead, coat with steel, attach with chain to man's penis. Attach a blunt knife to it, throw into sea. 'Odd Job' it through the air and knock off head.

Another fifteen-year-old, a specialist in history and English, also envisaged considerable atrocities. As himself, he had offered:

A POT OF JAM: Catching wasps in, with jam – getting your hand stuck in – putting marmalade in – throwing at trees – drinking out of – using it as a water container whilst painting – putting red and black ants in, for a fight –

As McMice, he was altogether more outspoken:

JAR OF TREACLE: Putting in people's eyes, part of a mobile piece of art, for covering pound notes in, drowning mice in, holding them under by the tail, stopping up nostrils, putting in hair, pouring slowly down the Queen's cunt (Queen being held upside down in Bond Street).

The themes of these two young men are insistently sadistic or sexually aggressive; and the tone of the first boy's script is distinctly unsettling. They are unusual in their vigour, but not in the extent to which role-playing loosened their pens. What matters most, though, is the extreme flimsiness of the artifice which released these horrible thoughts. The boys all sat together, under what were effectively examination conditions, in their school hall, the portraits of former headmasters gazing down at them. The test instructions were a painfully contrived charade. Even so, they allowed many of the boys to disown responsibility for what they wrote. Some of their products are morsels from the witches' cauldron. The world is that of Peter's drawings; a seething morass of improprieties.

In Eve White, the control of unacceptable impulses was Draconian: she did not simply block or 'repress' them; she excluded them from herself altogether, and personified them as Eve Black. In the case of my schoolboys, it was more a matter of impulses being bottled up, or suppressed.

In making sense of either we move naturally into the frame of reference of the actor. For many theorists – most notably the sociologist, Erving Goffman – have argued that none of us is a single self; we are a whole repertoire of selves that bob up as occasion demands.[16] The person who steadfastly presents the same face to the world (and to himself) is, on this argument, simply someone in whom one self has successfully tyrannized all others. Goffman has gone on to argue that the faces we present to the world are not really faces at all, but masks. All day and every day, we act parts for one another, using the repertoire that our culture provides. What lies behind each mask is a void; or, rather, the simple desire to get on with people, the need to be accepted and confirmed.

Goffman's metaphor of man as the empty actor has proved beguiling. It saves so much fuss. Like Skinner's doctrine of behaviourism, his scheme promises to resolve the philosophical ambiguities and the technical difficulties of psychology at a stroke. And its appeal is heightened by Goffman's great shrewdness as an analyst of 'face work' – the games we play in order to create the desired impression in those around us. But by now we should be alert to the games that psychologists and sociologists play too, and ready to unpack their covert implications. Even at this short distance in time, Goffman's metaphor seems a little dated: reminiscent of Whyte's 'Organisation Man', and an ap-

16. Goffman (1959). His writing has been influential on a whole school of 'symbolic interactionist' sociologists – for instance, Strauss (1969) and Manis and Meltzer (1967) – and also on psychiatrists like Laing (1960).

propriate commentary on the commercial life of the 1950s rather than a recipe for Man more generally.

It should give us pause, too, that many professional actors themselves do not subscribe to the Goffmanesque model. In the course of his much maligned biographical study of Marilyn Monroe, Norman Mailer distinguishes between the European 'Coquelin' and the American 'Method' schools of acting – the first being close to Goffman's conception, the other not.[17] The Coquelin school Mailer describes as being 'external', encouraging the actor, in effect, to impersonate. This approach offers actors quick rewards, allowing them to move painlessly from one part to another. Also, more personally, it provides them with a protective 'armor' – one which enables them, in Mailer's phrase, 'to contain the shapelessness of their psyches'. On the other hand, it can be seen as a technique that encourages the actor 'to become more skillfully phony'. The Method school, in contrast, invites the actor to begin with what is 'internal', and then to 'act out': '. . . their technique is designed, like psychoanalysis itself, to release emotional lava, and thereby enable the actor to become acquainted with his depths, then possess them enough to become possessed by his role'.[18]

An obvious drawback of this approach is that it is inconvenient, leaving the actor ill-equipped to cope with parts that are alien or meretricious: 'The worse the role, the more one needs an external style . . . Living with the wrong part is like living with the wrong mate and having to make love every night.'

However, the world of actors does not divide itself neatly between Coquelin and Method; 'external' and 'internal'. Many gifted character actors do give the impression that they have drawerfuls of ready-made characters stored in their mental antechambers, instantly on tap. But others claim that they work themselves only slowly into a part, locating aspects of their own experience that correspond, more or less approximately, to what the playwright has written. Eileen Atkins has recently had this to say about her part in Marguerite Duras' play, *The Square*:

17. Mailer (1974). Accusations of plagiarism have obscured the real merits of this essay. His is one of the most sophisticated analyses I have seen of the difficulties inherent in any attempt to reconstruct the life of a public figure, especially where this is shrouded in what Mailer calls 'factoids' – consciously manufactured myths.

18. Mailer (1974), p. 108.

I find this play the most exposing thing I have ever played. It's about something every woman knows about. She has had twenty years with a man who's still got a terrific hold on her, but it's dead. It's not doing either of you any good any more and you see something else that's possible, and you're between them, and you're torn, and it's agony . . . This part is an ordinary woman stuck between two men. I've got nothing to hide behind. It's extremely emotional – the most screwing up part. It's like taking a knife right down the middle of you and saying 'This is how I feel'. I always feel very peaceful after I've done it.

I only know that I always feel when I'm starting a part that there's a rod inside me that's absolutely covered with barnacles. Because you see so many things, and it's always a mess, and you are not sure why you say that at that particular point. But by the time you come to the first night, you've got to have a shining piece of steel down the centre of you that's got a shape . . . If there's still a barnacle on the rod, I'll go at it and at it. I've spent three or four hours with two words because they didn't work. I know they're not coming out, and it's not until they're absolutely rooted in you that you're just saying them, and it's not until it looks easy that it's right.[19]

There is little trace here of the donning and doffing of masks. Quite the reverse, in fact. Parts like this offer the actor the chance to order her own experience and utter it; and to do so in ways that are quite exceptionally exposed. The part is an opportunity she takes to discover who she is and what she can become. The processes whereby a gifted actor or actress discovers a memorable interpretation, and those whereby a gifted novelist or playwright establishes a memorable character would seem to have much in common. And both – as Norman Mailer suggests – have more in common than one might imagine with the task of the biographer, especially when he begins to penetrate beneath the skin of facts (and 'factoids') that his subject offers. All three are processes of re-creation, in which the individual draws on his own intuitive resources but must do so in ways that satisfy the external constraints that role, plot or biographical information represent.[20]

There is, then, an inadequacy about Goffman's conception of man as an empty actor. Frequently, he illuminates the processes whereby we survive in social situations, and does so convincingly. But he tells us nothing credible about the internal architecture of the creature who is doing the surviving. In this

19. Atkins (1973), p. 9.
20. Hudson (1975).

respect, his view is inferior to that provided by the octagons in Chapter 4. In retrospect, the glamour and elan of Goffman's thinking owes a great deal to the fiercely reductive nature of the redefinition of reality he attempts. But his redrawing *is* reductive; and the kinds of research it fosters stress our capacity to manipulate and deceive, while leaving, at the heart of the matter, a conceptual and moral vacuum. And it is just this space that psychological theory should be designed to fill.

In attempting to fill it, we would be unwise, certainly, to slip to the other extreme, and to think of authentic utterance as a matter of unleashing primitive instincts that layers of civilizing convention have obscured. Rather, it is a business of exploiting these conventions in ways which make the symbolic expression of our needs possible. The choice, in other words, is one between utterances of ourselves that are more or less gratifyingly eloquent. This eloquence is something we achieve only by means that are in one way or another symbolic – and when we achieve it, we do so in the teeth of our own mixed feelings. But to suggest that it cannot occur – or that it cannot occur in varying degrees – seems to me a superficiality that psychologists should ignore.

Part Three

Patterns of Development

8 The Origins of Need

Unlike the lowlier forms of life – the rat, stickleback or cuckoo – human beings take shape only slowly. Our responses are more diverse, and more adaptable. Specialists in animal behaviour, like Konrad Lorenz, urge us to believe that despite this appearance of variety and flexibility the human is like the stickleback after all. Both his individual needs and his patterns of social organization represent the expression of 'instincts'; of a genetic programme that needs only to be triggered by environmental stimuli.[1] This essentially speculative vision is countered by another: the social scientist's conviction that all important causes are cultural; a matter of 'mores' and 'norms'. Where one school of thought assumes that we are quite rigidly constrained by our biological destiny, our 'biogrammar', the other holds to a determinism that is cultural or economic. Like the debates of theologians, this one proves, over and again, to rest on a sea of muddles and misconceptions. In looking at the evidence we possess about human development, it is an irrelevance.

At the risk of seeming heavily didactic, there are some simple distinctions that I want to put forward before looking at any developmental evidence at all. These are of the kind that all psychologists pay lip-service to, but forget as soon as a juicy morsel of evidence hoves in view. If we ask why some people are, say, more aggressive than others, we must be light enough on our feet to see that we are asking two sorts of question in one. We are asking, in the first place, a question about origins or aetiology. And we are asking a question about the function of such a disposition, once it is established, in maintaining the internal equilibrium of the individual. Each of these questions – about *origins* and about *psychological function* – is distinct from a third: that, namely, about the biographical *consequences* of such a

1. Lorenz (1966); also, more polemically, Tiger and Fox (1972).

characteristic. That is to say, about its effects on the life the person will actually lead. And each of these three questions invites answers of its own characteristic variety – as Figure 11 shows.

Confusion between these three different sorts of question arises in its crudest form around evidence that is genetic. If a psychologist asserts that such-and-such a human characteristic is inherited, that it is 'wired in' at birth and is part of our 'bio-grammar', both he and his opponents often go on to assume that all other questions about this characteristic are trivial: that debate about it has in effect been short-circuited. But to demonstrate that a difference in disposition is hereditarily determined is to say nothing one way or the other, either about the psychological function of such a difference or about its biographical consequences. It does not even tell us whether a risk-taking person, for example, might not become timid in some new social context; nor whether a similar result might not be achieved by some tampering with his brain chemistry.

In other words, psychological interpretations of development often address more than one category of explanation at a time. Logically, though, these categories remain separate. Each defines a legitimate area for research; and all three are worth exploring, the second and third perhaps more than the first.

In an effort to establish a basic model of human development, many psychologists have looked, very reasonably, towards biology. At present, there are only the barest threads to work with; but although the relation between human biology and the more complex aspects of human experience has been neglected, a resurgence of interest seems on the way.

Two spheres of research activity have a particular bearing on the themes of this book: the structure and function of the brain, and the physiological basis of need – especially sexual need. Both are fields of the profoundest interest, and although evidence is beginning to accumulate, we are still, in both cases, very much at sea. It is important, therefore, that we should be clear straight away, about what we know.

Consider, first, the mysteries of brain-damage: the historic case, for example, of Phineas Gage. Phineas was a foreman, a healthy, active and responsible 25-year-old working on a railway in Vermont. One day in 1848 an accidental explosion blew a crowbar up through his face and out of the top of his head. This large missile, smoothed with use, was three foot seven inches in length, an inch and a quarter in diameter, and weighed thirteen and a quarter pounds. It passed through his left cheek, and out through the top of his skull. Phineas, carried on an ox-cart to his hotel, was able to get out of the cart himself with only a little assistance; and an hour or so later he walked up a long flight of stairs. Weakened by the haemorrhage from his wound, he none the less remained fully conscious.

Eventually, he recovered; physically at least. However, all was not well. His doctor gives us the following account of him:

The equilibrium or balance, so to speak, between his intellectual faculties and animal propensities, seems to have been destroyed. He is fitful, irreverent, indulging at times in the grossest profanity (which was not previously his custom), manifesting but little deference for his fellows, impatient of restraint or advice when it conflicts with his desires, at times pertinaciously obstinate, yet capricious and vacillating, devising many plans of future operations, which are no sooner arranged than they are abandoned in turn for others appearing more feasible. A child in his intellectual capacity and manifestations, he has the animal passions of a strong man . . . In this regard his mind is radically changed, so decidedly that his friends and acquaintances said he was 'no longer Gage'.[2]

The part of his brain destroyed was the part that distinguishes the brain of a man most obviously from that of an ape: the frontal lobes. On the strength of evidence about war wounds, and of more carefully induced damage in operations performed on the frontal lobes of mental patients, we know that surprisingly large areas of this uniquely human grey matter can be disconnected or destroyed with comparatively little effect. As with Phineas, the patients' powers of imaginativeness, initiative and discretion often seem disrupted; but unlike him, they seem virtually unimpaired in their ability, for example, to do an I.Q. test.[3]

We also know that skills lost through damage to one area of the brain can sometimes be recovered, another area taking over

2. Taken from Coleman (1956), p. 447.
3. On the other hand, they do appear to become more rigid, losing their ability to switch from one principle of classification to another, and also their capacity to cope with open-ended tasks like the Uses of Objects test: Zangwill (1970).

First Question:	what is its *origin*?
Some typical answers:	It's inherited
	It's caused by inadequate mothering
	It's the product of social expectation
	It's an effect of hormonal imbalance during pregnancy

Second Question:	what is its *psychological function*?
Some typical answers:	It holds anxiety at bay
	It gratifies the appetite for power
	It reconciles incompatible beliefs
	It sublimates sexual desire

Third Question:	what is its biographical *consequence*?
Some typical answers:	It causes shyness
	It fosters conservative attitudes
	It leads to special skill in arithmetic
	It increases the risk of divorce

Figure 11. The development of any given human characteristic: the three basic issues

the destroyed tissue's function. And we know, from drastic surgical attempts to control epilepsy, that it is possible to slice the whole brain in two, from front to back, yet create in these 'split brain' patients impairments of reasoning relatively so subtle that careful experiments are required to detect them.[4] These 'split brain' studies lend some support to the view that one cerebral hemisphere, usually the left, is predominantly concerned with verbal and analytical thinking, while the other is more implicated in intuitive thought and in the reasoning we do in terms of patterns and shapes.[5] More generally, we know that specific areas of the brain have specific functions; that, for example, there is an area at the back of the brain that deals with information coming from the eye.[6] On the other hand, we do not in the least understand the working principles of these areas – nor, at present, have we much idea how to find these out.

If we turn from the study of the brain's structure and function to that of our hormones – and, specifically, of our sex hormones – a similarly tantalizing air of puzzlement surrounds us. It is hard to be categorical in such matters, especially as an outsider, but, contrary to popular assumption, there appears at present to be no binding evidence that our sex hormones directly control our sexual desires. Tempting inferences, yes; but hard evidence, no. We know that adults differ to quite remarkable extents in the amounts of sex hormone they secrete, some people's bloodstreams containing twenty or thirty times as much of certain sex hormones as do others.[7] Also that levels of sex hormone fluctuate sharply within the individual from time to time – the most remarkable of these occurring in mothers whilst pregnant and giving birth. But these differences do not parallel changes in mood or need in any simple or straightforward way. The nearest we get to direct evidence of a relation between hormonal secretions and sexual behaviour comes from the field of surgery. It is vital, though, that we bear in mind the gross mutilations that are inflicted on the people concerned in this work. If a person has been subjected to major surgery of any kind, especially surgery

4. Sperry (1964), Zangwill (1974).
5. Levy-Agresti and Sperry (1968). Zangwill (1974) makes the interesting observation that the position of the 'split-brain' patient is 'not unlike that of the automatic writer or the performer of a post-hypnotic suggestion'.
6. Hubel (1963).
7. Williams (1963).

affecting symbolically conspicuous parts of the body, or that makes him realize that his life is in danger, the subsequent alterations in his behaviour cannot be considered in purely physical terms.

There are indications from Danish experiments in the castration of male sex-offenders that this drastic manœuvre frequently diminishes men's sexual appetites to more socially convenient levels.[8] But as far as causes are concerned, the evidence is obviously equivocal. In some ways more vivid are the reports of changes that occur in the lives of women as a result of the removal of their ovaries and adrenal glands. This operation has been performed on women with breast cancer, because it was believed that the malignancies were sustained by hormonal secretions from the glands in question.[9] After the operation, such women were dosed with those cortico-steroids necessary to maintain life, but were left without the chief sex hormones: the oestrogens and androgens. The indications were that the removal of their androgens created in these women an abrupt and definitive loss of sexual desire and sexual responsiveness.

One woman whose sexual life until that point had been 'entirely satisfactory', had the operation in two stages, losing first her ovaries and then her adrenal gland. After losing her ovaries she retained a 'strong feeling for the difference between the sexes', but after the removal of the adrenal gland, she became 'completely neutral'. An 'onlooker', she felt 'quite serene and at peace with the world'; but quite 'content to see life sail by and take no part in it'. She was no longer a sexual entity. Another woman describes a sharp, and to her unexpected, change in her desire for her husband: she wanted to be close to him, and loved him still, but she experienced no sexual pleasure whatever.

Obviously, nothing much can be built on the experiences of a handful of late-middle-aged women, subject to gross surgical mutilation. None the less, it does seem as if the intimate needs of these women have a number of component parts, some under the control of their sex hormones, others not. 'Love' remains;

8. Sturup (1971).
9. Drellich and Waxenberg (1966). What is not clear is the extent to which the changes they report could prove explicable in other terms: as resulting, for instance, from the removal of the patients' breasts.

also the desire to 'nestle' near a protective and reassuring presence. On the other hand, sexual desire and the capacity to have an orgasm are expunged; likewise that much more delicate tension with which social relationships between men and women are ordinarily endowed.

There is also evidence – again shaky, but intriguing – that sex hormones influence the patterns of intelligence that we display. The menstrual cycle, for example, appears to influence the intellectual risks that women take – making them more cautious during the second half of the cycle, more likely to take risks during the first.[10] And, altogether more speculative, there is now a popular line of argument that connects sex hormones and intelligence in a developmental fashion. Individuals' oestrogen/androgen balance has been linked to their preference for verbal as opposed to non-verbal reasoning – though in practice the web of inference here proves tangled.[11] And more remarkably, other studies have suggested that spatial reasoning may be especially weak in women afflicted with Turner's syndrome – a genetic defect involving their sex chromosomes, and adversely affecting their sexual development.[12] And, more remarkably still, there is evidence that can be construed as showing that sex hormones administered to mothers can produce long-term and beneficial effects on the intelligence of their children.[13]

All evidence of this sort produced to date can either be destroyed on methodological grounds, or reinterpreted from a psychological or sociological rather than a biological point of view.[14] However, the engines of research are only just beginning to turn; and what are now somewhat fanciful interpretations of fragile evidence may quite rapidly harden. It would, after all, be odd if biology had nothing to contribute to the personal differences between adults.

*

10. Cormack and Sheldrake (1974).
11. Bock (1973).
12. Money (1970). The argument here, though, is quite exceptionally precarious; see Hudson (1971).
13. Dalton (1968). Studies with monkeys tell an analogous story, injections of male sex hormone in the pregnant mother leading to female offspring whose behaviour is tomboyish: Young, Goy and Phoenix (1964).
14. Hudson (1971).

For a paragraph or two, we have been on thin ice. You realize, when you look in detail, that we know surprisingly little about the physical bases either of human intelligence, or of human need. It is only when we turn to the cultural context which shapes the expression of our needs that the ice thickens, and we have the sense of solid evidence beneath our feet. This evidence, again about sex and gender, is in part anthropological. While anthropological evidence reveals an astounding variety of social organization and custom, there exist, running through this evidence of diversity, two obvious regularities. Both are pertinent. The first concerns the sex typing of behaviour: the fact that certain activities, the world over, are predominantly the preserve of men, while others are predominantly the preserve of women. The second concerns the incest taboo; the rules that all societies evolve, in order to prevent sexual relationships between members of the same family. Together, these two regularities constitute what we might call – in the great variety of its forms – the 'sexual organization of family life'.

D'Andrade, in a review of evidence about several hundred primitive societies, found, overwhelmingly, that the upbringing of boys tended to stress self-reliance and achievement; while that of girls stressed nurturance, responsibility and obedience.[15] He also found that in all primitive societies, it is the men who hunt, and the men who wage war. Conversely, it is almost always the women who cook, carry water, grind grain.

On the face of it, these differences may seem to spring from difference of physique; but in truth they are at least in part symbolic. For while weapon-making is almost exclusively a male preserve, the bearing of burdens is more often an activity of women than men – yet it is the bearing of burdens that demands the more strength. There is a sense, in other words, in which men dominate weapon-making because of the symbolic associations that weapon-making possesses. Likewise with the bearing of burdens, an activity judged appropriate to the menial position in primitive societies that women usually occupy.

The women of primitive societies look to their children and to their husbands; while their men look outward to the security of the group as a whole. This simple postural arrangement, morally

15. D'Andrade (1970). Most anthropologists, it must be admitted, view such cross-cultural comparisons with alarm.

deplorable though it may seem, is one neatly captured in an analysis of the dreams reported by members of seventy-five tribal societies. Colby found that a wife was four times as likely to dream about her husband, as her husband was to dream about her.[16]

So much for economically primitive societies. What of more sophisticated ones? And what, particularly, of efforts made by the civilized to redress these sexual inequalities? The best evidence is that from the Israeli kibbutzim, because these were communities set up explicitly to avoid discrimination by sex. Initially, men and women alike drove tractors, cooked food and looked after the children. Evidence conflicts, but some commentators insist that despite these good intentions, a polarization would seem to have occurred spontaneously. There is a tendency for men to specialize in the technical and mechanical aspects of kibbutz life; while women are the more likely to concern themselves primarily with cooking, laundering and bringing up the children.[17]

As in the kibbutzim, so in other sophisticated cultures. There are activities in European and American societies – engineering, for instance – that are almost entirely the preserve of men. In the British Isles as recently as the 1950s, only 1 professional mechanical engineer in every 1,500 was a woman.[18] As before, this massive differentiation reflects not the actual capacities of men and women, which are found in any sample to overlap to a very considerable extent, but the symbolic significance of the activities in question. For reasons that we do not yet wholly understand, professional engineering – like hi-fi, photography, and tinkering with internal combustion engines – is seen as quintessentially 'male'. Nursing and primary-school teaching are seen as 'female'. These are systems of preconceptions to which biological and cultural influences contribute. They determine the roles in society men and women are free to play; and they are less easy to alter than they might at first seem.

16. Summarized by D'Andrade (1970). The other qualities more likely to crop up in male dreams than in female ones were all of symbolic significance: 'grass', 'coitus', 'weapon', 'animal', 'death'. Those more likely to crop up in female dreams than male ones were equally eloquent: 'clothes', 'mother', 'father', 'child', 'home'.
17. See, for example, Spiro (1956).
18. Klein (1966).

To be a female engineer is to be something out of the ordinary. But not illegal. In this respect, the definition of sex roles and the incest taboo differ sharply. For sexual relationships within the immediate family, between brothers and sisters, or parents and children, is not merely unusual in the statistical sense; it is viewed with repugnance, and frequently punished in the most violent ways.[19]

There are exceptions, of course; but they are hard to find. Occasionally, societies have permitted incestuous relationships among their most privileged groups: in Ancient Peru the Incas married their sisters, while among the Ptolemys of Ancient Egypt almost every kind of intra-family marriage was practised, and the brother assumed his regal prerogatives through marrying his sister. Among the Dierri tribesmen, it is said, incest was permitted on the eve of battle to 'arouse the warriors to a proper emotional pitch'. But these instances are rare; and in the vast majority of societies that prohibit incest, transgressions are very much the territory of the misfit.[20]

Families in our own society in which incest occurs are either extremely close-knit, and cut off from other social contacts; or so loosely organized as scarcely to constitute a family at all. Occasionally, sects cut themselves off – as sometimes a single family does – from the values of society as a whole. The Mormons positively encouraged marriages that were both polygamous and incestuous; and Weinberg tells of one involving three women of direct descent: grandmother, mother and daughter, all three sleeping together with the husband, with children of all ages, in a single room. Such goings-on are, however, quite out of the ordinary run.

Family life is organized the world over, then, both by sex and by gender. Boys and girls learn, usually quite explicitly, that certain activities are judged appropriate to them, others inappropriate. They also learn – more covertly – that their amorous impulses can only be satisfied outside the family. These two messages can be said to constitute the 'deep structure' of family life: the pattern on which it tacitly depends.

19. In the cross-cultural study on which D'Andrade drew, Murdock concluded that in not one of 250 societies was it permissible for father and daughter, mother and son, or brother and sister to have sexual intercourse or to marry.
20. Weinberg (1955).

We do not wholly understand, yet, why we are so zealous in our differentiation of sex roles; nor why we prohibit incestuous relationships with such vigour. The incest taboo has been explained, severally, as a biological mechanism to avoid inbreeding; and as a social mechanism to foster alliances between families who would otherwise live in mutual isolation. Neither line of interpretation is convincing. But whatever its explanation, it is certain that the incest taboo serves a powerfully expulsive function. Each of us is launched out into the world in search of a soul's mate, and along a path that is sharply constrained by gender. We go either as a male, or as a female. When the individual is 'expelled' from the nuclear family in search of a habitable identity, it is his sense of *gender* – his 'masculinity' or 'femininity' – that is the first constraint on the path he follows.

From work with small children whose gender has been falsely ascribed – boys treated as girls, girls brought up as boys – we know that the individual's sense of his or her own masculinity or femininity is firmly established by the age of two-and-a-half or three. To attempt to shift it thereafter is to risk major psychic upheaval.[21]

In bygone days, when the differentiation of the sexes in our own society was particularly fierce, we were content to overlook the subtle distinctions that these words 'masculinity' and 'femininity' hide. If you were a man, it was 'natural' that you should be attracted to women; if a woman, to men. Men attracted to men, women attracted to women, men who wanted to be women, women who thought they were men – all these were explained away as degenerates. One of the most significant consequences of Freud's work has been our greater willingness to explore these mid-ground states, and to realize that they are not as remote from the experience of ordinary men and women as they once seemed.

First, we need some distinctions. Stoller draws some of these neatly for us in his book *Sex and Gender*.[22] He distinguishes the *object* of sexual desire (in the homosexual male, another man); from the desire to *be* someone (in the effeminate male, the desire to be a woman). Both these he distinguishes from the conviction we all feel about our sexual identity: that we are male or female.

21. Money *et al.* (1957).
22. Stoller (1968).

Slippage between these three categories produces a number of quite different predicaments.

The heterosexual man, if we may take males as our starting point, acknowledges his biological nature, and desires women ('I, a male, want her'). The 'masculine' homosexual also acknowledges his maleness, but desires other men ('I, a male, want him'). The heterosexually effeminate man is the one who desires women, and to some extent identifies with them. He is, phenomenologically speaking, a lesbian ('I, a male, both want her, and want to be like her'). The effeminate homosexual again acknowledges that he is a man, would like to be a woman, but desires other men ('I, a male, would like to be her, and want him'). The trans-sexual male is someone who – like the writer James Morris – is convinced beyond all reasoning, and beyond the evidence of biology, that he is a woman, not a man ('I, a male, *am* her').

This, however, is only a beginning. Our masculinity or femininity expresses itself equally in our choice of work and interests, and also in our social manner or style. We have, for example, the male transvestite: someone compelled to take on the outward signs of femininity, although without abandoning his sense of his own maleness ('I, a male, want to look like her'). Masculinity and femininity have then, at the very minimum, five elements: our biological nature; our sense of our maleness or femaleness ('gender identity'); the choice we make of a sexual object; our social manner; and our choice of work and interests – and their attendant assumptions and habits of mind. And this is not an idle piece of list-making, because perceived incongruities between these various layers of masculinity or femininity can become both a source of anguish, and the driving force on which a way of life depends.

How are such choices made? The conventional wisdom of the textbooks is that they are made through the processes of 'socialization' and 'identification', and that they are determined by a wide variety of precipitating circumstances, not just one. Such verbal formulae offer the illusion of intellectual mastery, without its substance. The truth is that we do not understand what is afoot. We *know* that children are 'socialized': that is to say, induced into the assumptions and values of their society. We *know* that they 'identify' with significant others in their lives –

not simply imitating them, but using them as models on which to base their sense of who they are. But to say this is to say little. What we need is some more specific sense of the nature of the pressures that parents exert, and of the kinds of result this pressure achieves.

The virtue of Stoller's case studies lies in their vivid particularity. They also jolt us into realizing on what a slender basis of intuitive judgment our assumptions about sexual normality rest.

One case concerns a mother in her forties and her five-year-old son. She is described as 'perky, charming, and sharply alert . . . younger than her age . . . like one of the flippant, intelligent movie stars who in the last generation have portrayed a boyish femininity in which soft sweetness covers a capacity to outdo the masculine bluster of men'. She, on the other hand, describes herself as empty: 'nothing, a cipher, a mirage'. Everyone who saw her son seems to have agreed that he was a 'lovely-looking, charming, witty, brilliant, warm, sensitive, altogether winning child'. At school his proficiency as a dancer was so great that a professional film had been made of him. Like his mother, he seemed quite exceptionally sensitive to colours, textures, materials.

Her husband is described as conventionally masculine; but, as the mother describes herself, as empty. The relation between husband and wife was one of hatred, it seems: she threw chairs, and he, passive, removed himself both physically and spiritually from the home for long periods. There was also a daughter, older than the son, about whom Stoller says little. Their son had been a planned baby, although at the time of conception the mother's distaste for her husband was already fully fledged. Her claim was that she 'had to have a baby'. There was no thought, though, of using the baby to save the marriage, as she felt no desire for separation or divorce. For both partners, the proper balance in marriage would seem to have been a mixed sense of emptiness and dislike.

The son of this marriage dressed himself as a girl. This predilection in its turn seems to have sprung from the intense preoccupation that he shared with his mother for clothes; and also from the curious degree of physical intimacy she had established with him. She had herself grown up longing to be a boy; and as a compromise with her own female appurtenances, had settled for sexual neutrality: a boy-like woman.[23] Her young son she saw as a cure for her sense of emptiness. She enjoyed her pregnancies, and enjoyed close physical contact with her son. She talked of him as though he were not a child but a complete equal; one she found profound delight in. Her physical contact with him seems virtually to have been continuous: 'he was permitted to share her body with her as though it was his own. This was not experienced by either as heterosexual, but was rather the same sort of unselfconscious freedom one has with one's own body, unencumbered by excitement, curiosity, hostility, or shame.' Stoller records two eloquent anecdotes from the mother:

When he was an infant, if he was restless or had the hiccups, I'd roll up my pyjama top, roll down his diapers and lay him on my abdomen. It always quieted him.

This morning I was in the bathroom undressed. He came in while I was facing backwards and didn't know he was there and slapped me on the fanny and said with a laugh, 'What a lovely butt.' I laughed and told him how cute he was.[24]

This mother evidently has contrived to circumvent the normal cultural rules that ensure a degree of distance – both physical, and in identification – between a mother and her son. The intimacy between them was profound; and the consequence, if unusual, by no means wholly calamitous. A strange and in some ways gifted woman, she may well have produced a strange and in some ways gifted son.

The psychic life of the child seems to echo or complement the psychic life of the parent. As Erikson once pointed out in a memorable phrase, the neurotic symptoms of the child reflect its mother's deepest conflict.[25] It is not simply patterns of behaviour that are transmitted, but patterns in the management of impulse, of need.

23. Her own mother, it seems, was 'hollow' too. And her father, an alcoholic, was a man 'who displayed two distinct personalities, the one a happy, humorous, singing, very affectionate father; the other, a man of terrifying violence and scarcely veiled sexuality during the frequent times he was drunk'.
24. Stoller (1968), p. 111.
25. Erikson (1963), p. 30.

Another of Stoller's cases casts light on this process of trans-
mission; and does so from an adjacent but subtly different position. This again concerns a married woman; here, with two
pre-adolescent sons. She was bisexual. Desperately wanting to
be a boy when she was young, she too suffered a sense of emptiness. On the other hand, she had a vigorously ambiguous sex
life; yet was scrupulously careful not to transmit to her sons her
own bisexual vision. She describes how, quite consciously, she
kept such feelings at bay when she was with her infants.

Equally interesting – a different but related issue – is the split
nature of her sexual expression:

I never felt masculine while having sexual relations with a man. I had
a very satisfying time sexually with men and still do. When I'm having
sexual relations with a woman I can feel completely masculine, as long
as she doesn't touch me in the pubic area. No matter what sexual
activity I'm engaged in with a woman I always have an orgasm when
she has one, and this can occur without my genitals having been
touched. During my sexual relationship with a woman I actually feel
as though I have a penis. I feel totally masculine and superior to the
female I'm with. When I experience an orgasm I feel that I ejaculate
. . . My orgasm is not a single feeling but more of a spasmodic sensation. I can have sexual relations with a woman, have one orgasm and be
completely satisfied. When I have intercourse with a man I have to
have several orgasms before I can relax and feel satisfied.[26]

We learn something here about the complexity of desire: a
sense of layer on layer that the congruence of ordinary heterosexual relations obscures. If this woman is with a man, she sees
herself as submissive; if with a woman, as dominant. If she is
submissive, she has multiple orgasms; if dominant, a single
orgasm.[27] So while her desire for a particular man or woman is
an idea that must, in some sense and at some stage, have been
shaped by a physical need, the form of that physical expression
is governed by her perception of those persons and her relation
to them. The hydraulic engineer's language of energy flows and
outlets is quite inadequate here. For while the symbolic apparatus of desire – the attraction to particular kinds of men or
women, and the sense of being dominant or submissive to them

26. Stoller (1968), p. 173.
27. We have no psychologically literate account of such phenomena. For the
physiology, see Masters and Johnson (1966).

– is fashioned from the raw materials of physical desire, it is that apparatus in its turn which governs the way in which physical desire is expressed. Sexual intercourse, in other words, is a highly cerebral activity, not least for those most robustly physical in their sense of what they are doing.

9 Frames of Mind

'Expelled' by the incest taboo, and the Oedipal tensions it creates, focused by the definition of ourselves as male or female, we each grow up to create for ourselves a predominant disposition or frame of mind. This underlies the 'character' by which we are known; and it is within this that our more specific beliefs and skills are set.

Some of the most successful of research on the origins of the frames of mind of adolescents and adults has been that taking the greatest intellectual risks. Excellent results are now flowing, for example, as we shall see, from studies relating quite prosaic features of family structure to particular mental accomplishments.

This chapter describes a number of these studies, each of which throws light on the bases of our frames of mind; and, at the beginning of the next chapter, I will use this evidence to support a speculative model of psychological development – the 'fixation hypothesis'. Much of the evidence deals with factors acting on the child during the early years of his life. This selection is in part a reflection of my own interests; in part it has been directed by the evidence – psychoanalytic and statistical – suggesting that these years are in fact profoundly influential.[1]

But before looking at this evidence, there is a point of logic to sort out. Much of the material in this chapter interprets the lives of individuals on the basis of evidence about groups. This research is easily misconstrued – among others, by those conducting it – as an attempt to divide human beings into two or more subspecies: the choleric as opposed to the phlegmatic, melan-

1. Bloom (1964) argues on purely statistical grounds that 50 per cent of the variance that adolescents display in terms of their aggression, their dependency and the intellectuality of their interests can be predicted by the age of five.

cholic or sanguine; the introvert as opposed to the extrovert; the converger as opposed to the diverger; and so on. The error here is one of over-simplification. If we establish, as often happens in research, that half a dozen variables go together, in that they all correlate positively in a sample taken as a whole, there is then a strong temptation to treat this pattern as a 'syndrome' – a set of characteristics that will always crop up together. If we establish that men who vote Conservative also tend to be, say, friendly, anxious, weak-willed, to sleep poorly, and to be conscientious over their mortgage payments, we slip easily into the assumption that all Conservatives will have all of these characteristics.

Yet we know that this must be a blunder. Everyday experience tells us that people do not run to type in this way. If they did, we would treat them as zombies. Also, the logic of probability ensures that if there exist moderate degrees of correlation between half a dozen variables, only a few members of the sample will possess all six characteristics.[2]

To envisage such clusterings of human characteristics, you need an appropriate model. A humble but useful one is that of the solitaire board: a surface on which you can set up flat arrays of marble-like spheres. Each board, on this analogy, represents a person, and each marble a characteristic. If, for the sake of convenience, these characteristics can be limited to those (like conservative and radical) defined in terms of opposites, each marble can be coloured half black and half white, and the extent to which an individual tends to one or other extreme is conveyed by the extent to which the marble has its black or white side uppermost. If there are sound statistical or theoretical reasons for treating certain characteristics as a cluster, it is perfectly legitimate to estimate the over-all blackness or whiteness of each person's array: to show that, on the whole, he belongs to one type rather than another. But in doing this, it is vital that we bear in mind the inconsistencies that such averages hide – for it is these as much as his consistencies that will govern what the individual's reactions will be.[3]

2. This simple point is consistently overlooked in statistical textbooks.
3. It is also legitimate to envisage solitaire boards arranged hierarchically, so that each marble at any one level represents the average blackness or whiteness of the whole array in a level below it. This shift down from the macro- to the micro-cosmic is conceptually helpful, because in practice it is almost

With the solitaire board firmly in mind, we can begin to sift the evidence. The first piece springs from a most imaginative retrospective analysis which was carried out by a research student at Harvard, Lyn Carlsmith.[4] She realized that the Second World War constituted a natural experiment, in which large numbers of young husbands had gone off to fight, leaving behind them wives and infant sons. Many of these fathers safely returned. There was none the less a gap in their sons' experience; a space of months or years in which they had been fatherless. Now there is a tendency for women in our culture to show a bias of ability towards reasoning in terms of words, whereas men show a bias towards reasoning in terms of numbers. Carlsmith argued that if boys grow up to be masculine because they identify with their fathers, those with absent fathers would be more girl-like, and would lack the characteristically male bias towards mathematical reasoning.

It sounds a very long shot; but it worked. Carlsmith took the class of 1964 at Harvard, looked up their scores on the Scholastic Aptitude Test, and compared their verbal scores with their mathematical scores. She then matched two groups of students, 20 in each. The first was of students whose fathers had been away for at least two years during the subjects' infancies, and had then permanently returned. The other was of students from similar social backgrounds, whose fathers had stayed at home. Eighteen out of the 20 in the 'father-present' group had the typical male bias towards the mathematical part of the S.A.T.; only 7 out of the 20 in the 'father-absent' group did so. Rather, their S.A.T. scores looked like those of highly intelligent young women. Carlsmith found, too, that the earlier the father had left home, and the longer he was away, the more marked this effect became.

Carlsmith's research is not watertight, of course. Such research rarely can be. Her results encourage us to see the bond between father and son, and the early years, as crucial.[5] However, a husband's absence may exert a long-term influence over his

always possible to break a simple-looking human characteristic down into its constituent consistencies and inconsistencies.
4. Carlsmith (1970).
5. Vernon's (1969) studies of Jamaican, American Indian and Eskimo children tend to confirm this.

marriage – serving to intensify the bond between son and mother. On this argument, the crucial influence on the son could be exerted not in the first three years of life, but later on; and not by the father, but – as in Stoller's cases – by the mother.

A somewhat similar air of ambiguity hangs around all statistical evidence about upbringing. For instance, that on birth-order. Many years ago, Francis Galton pointed out that successful people were usually first-born or only sons. Famous scientists, politicians and scholars tended, and still tend, to be first-born. Subsequent research has supported Galton handsomely; and although efforts have been made to explain away the data in terms of social class, differential fertility and statistical muddles of various sorts, the effect remains. A study of over a thousand finalists in the National Merit competition in the United States showed, for example, that among these brilliantly successful students the first-born were consistently over-represented. Of the 568 from two-child families, two in every three were first-borns. Among the 85 from five-child families, more than half were first born – the other four birth-ranks contributing only 48 per cent between them.[6]

A deeply intriguing feature of this birth-order effect is that it appears to grow stronger the more highly selected on intellectual grounds the populations in question become. Among the very large numbers of students who took the first rounds of the National Merit tests, for example, the birth-order effects were slight or non-existent. But in her study of distinguished American scientists, Anne Roe found that no fewer than 72 per cent had been, in fact or effect, the oldest sons in their families.[7]

It seems that older and younger brothers also differ in personality. The psychoanalyst Alfred Adler once described the typical first born as 'a power-hungry conservative'; and, on the whole, the evidence seems to support him. Oldest sons seem to be more conscientious, too; and more carefully attuned to the requirements of adult society.[8]

6. Altus (1970). This effect appears to concern both sexes equally.
7. Roe (1953).
8. Altus (1970). A weakness of birth-order research, pointed out to me by Professor Franz Halberg, is that it usually contains no adequate control for the age of the mother. The mothers of first-borns are, on average, younger than those of later borns – and hence may differ in terms both of the pre- and post-natal environment they provide.

This evidence about primogeniture has been available for some time; and no one has quite known what to make of it. Recently, however, it has been put to work. Another Harvard research student, Frank Sulloway, has used it to cast new light on the psychology of those who take part in scientific revolutions.[9]

Most scientific revolutionaries – Newton, for example, and Einstein – are first-borns. But something strange happens when we look at the Darwinian revolution in biology. Sulloway shows that all of the famous men who were evolutionists, or who were quickly converted to Darwin's point of view, were – like Charles Darwin himself – *younger* brothers. Conversely, almost all of the eminent men who opposed the evolutionary doctrine were first-born or only sons.

Sulloway's suggestion is that the Darwinian revolution was unusual, in that it involved a radical shift in our conception of Man's place in Nature: we were shown to be descended from apes. The revolution was thus an 'emotional' one. Others in this category, Sulloway proposes, are the Copernican revolution in astronomy, in which the earth was displaced from the centre of the universe; and the Freudian revolution, in which Man was demoted from control of his own thoughts and deeds. Sulloway goes on to argue that the famous protagonists in these 'emotional' revolutions were almost all either younger brothers, or first-borns who were brought up to reject their fathers, or first-borns whose fathers were themselves revolutionaries.

Such historical analyses have their weaknesses and temptations. Biographical information about great men is usually saturated with the mythology of the hero; selected and biased by relatives, colleagues and biographers, each with a personal investment in conveying one impression rather than another. Even the best of the evidence is hard to read with any semblance of objectivity. Nevertheless, Sulloway's work establishes a valuable bridge where none previously existed; and does so in a way which unites unforeseen evidence with plausible theory in a most exciting way.[10]

9. Sulloway (1972).
10. This story contains a disconcerting twist. In Edinburgh, we have looked at both the Darwinian and the Einsteinian revolutions. The second, as Sulloway predicts, tends to follow the path of primogeniture: the majority of the participants, protagonists and antagonists alike, were first-born. But

An avenue towards slightly less far-flung patterns of inference lies in a pioneering study published by Jacob Getzels and Philip Jackson in the late 1950s.[11] This arose from their interest in creativeness; and, particularly, in the disposition to think creatively in science. They broke with a long-standing and stultifying tradition in mental measurement, and looked – as Carlsmith did – at students in terms of the biases of ability that each possessed. They distinguished two types of children: those who excelled at the conventional I.Q. test, but who were relatively poor at tests designed to measure their fluency and imaginativeness; and those with the reverse bias – highly fluent and imaginative, but with I.Q. scores which were relatively poor.

A great deal of work has subsequently been done with this distinction, some of it by myself; and the two types have come to be called 'convergers' and 'divergers' respectively.[12] Efforts have been made by the orthodox to discredit Getzels' and Jackson's work. The most absurd of these attempts has implied that convergers and divergers cannot really be different after all, because, when you perform statistical analyses on scores from the mental tests Getzels and Jackson used, both sorts of ability can be made to look like aspects of the same human attribute: 'general intelligence'.[13] While the profession's obscurantists pirouette on pins' heads in this engaging way, convergers and divergers continue stubbornly to differ. They differ in their personalities; and they differ in the kinds of brain work they are attracted to – convergers moving towards physical science, and divergers towards the humanities. In my own research I have found that convergers are more likely than divergers to show respect for authority, to adopt conventional attitudes, and to avoid the expression of humour or violence. They even differ, as we shall see, in the way they sleep and dream.

---

supporters and opponents of the relativity theory did differ in one respect; and it is, at first sight, a bizarre one. Most of those in favour were born in the winter; most of those opposed, in summer: Holmes (1974). The same proved to be true of the Darwinian revolution. Broadly, the 'revolutionaries' were winter-born, the 'conservatives' summer-born. Statistically most impressive, this finding has caused us to wonder in what respects the pre- and early post-natal environments of the summer- and winter-born child may differ: Halberg (1969), Dewan (1967), Wendt (1973).

11. Getzels and Jackson (1962), (1970).
12. Hudson (1966), (1968); Wallach and Kogan (1965).
13. See, for example, Burt (1962), Thorndike (1963).

A virtue of Getzels' and Jackson's research was their patience in scrutinizing the homes in which their convergers and divergers grew up. Convergers' mothers proved more highly educated, more critical of their children, and more anxious. Divergers' mothers, in contrast, were less well educated, more likely to go out to work, more accepting of their children. Getzels and Jackson even report that convergers' parents subscribed to more magazines than did divergers' – a difference that captures the convergers' parents greater concern with explicit improvement and instruction.[14]

However, most of Getzels' and Jackson's work, and evidence like it, rests on discriminations that are rather blurred. For every two or three instances that fit the argument, one runs the other way. Although such networks of correlation are worth assembling, they leave you at a distance from the vital issues of *psychological function*. To get to grips with these, you must look in more detail. Two studies are particularly eloquent in this respect; one on the expression of aggression, and the other on sleep and dreaming.

Looked at in bulk, divergers express more violent ideas on the Uses of Objects test than do convergers.[15] All-rounders, those with no clear bias, fall halfway between. On the other hand, these differences are small; in my studies, I found, in round figures, that the proportions producing violent ideas in the three groups were 50 per cent, 40 per cent and 33 per cent.

It dawned on me slowly that while most of the violent ideas put forward by divergers were mild, those from convergers were sometimes distinctly gruesome. Having assembled a working definition of 'extreme violence', I found that three times as many such responses were coming from convergers as from divergers. Figure 12 makes the point quite plainly: as mild violence goes up, extreme violence goes down; and vice versa.

The implication is that convergers are bottling up their aggression to a greater extent than divergers. It may well be, too, that the very process of bottling heightens the pressure in the bottle. The more effective the repression, the more turbulent the experiences repressed. Bottling may also lend to the violent ideas that convergers do express their quality of morbid elaboration.

14. Getzels and Jackson (1970).
15. Hudson (1966).

In expressing their violence, convergers are altogether more pent up than divergers: more specific; more personal; and – an important detail – more likely to refer to mothers, wives and sisters. Here are the five most violent suggestions to come from convergers in a large sample of schoolboys, and the equivalent number from divergers. These were produced under the normal

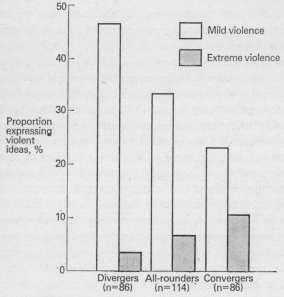

Figure 12. The expression of violent ideas among divergers, all-rounders and convergers

testing conditions: the boys in question were simply invited to write down whatever uses they saw fit.[16]

Violent Suggestions from Convergers
1. Smash sister's head in (Brick).
2. Wrap up dead wife so as blood doesn't stain car seats (Blanket).
3. To remove from baby sister's bed in mid-winter while asleep (Blanket).
4. To use (full of nails) to torture people (Barrel).
5. Suffocating a person to death (Blanket).

16. Hudson (1966).

Violent Suggestions from Divergers
1. Suicide (Paper Clip).
2. Murder by smothering (Blanket).
3. Nailing up one's study-mate inside (Barrel).
4. Unrefined torture (Paper Clip).
5. As a thumbscrew (Paper Clip).

The next piece in the jigsaw harks back to Chapter 6, and to the question of dreams. In some recent studies in Edinburgh, we have found that divergers are better than convergers at re-calling the content of their dreams.[17] If you select convergers and divergers from a sample of university undergraduates, and place them in a sleep laboratory, you find that, physiologically speaking, the convergers appear to dream more intensely – that is to say, they show a greater intensity of the rapid eye move-ments associated with dreaming.[18] Yet, if you wake both con-vergers and divergers in the midst of these rapid eye movement or REM periods, it is the divergers who are more likely to recall successfully. While divergers almost always recall, convergers fail on as many as 50 per cent of occasions – either recalling nothing, or remembering that they were dreaming but being unable to recall what their dreams were about. In other words, a high intensity of dreaming is associated with poor recall; low intensity with good recall.

Intriguingly, this advantage of divergers over convergers applies only to awakenings made when rapid eye movements are actually taking place. If awakenings are made in the gaps be-tween bursts of eye movement, both convergers and divergers recall well, the convergers being if anything the superior of the two. This discovery is an important one theoretically, because there is convincing evidence to suggest that it is the eye move-ments themselves that are associated with 'primary visual experience' – that is to say, with vivid visual images; whereas the gaps between bursts of eye movement are taken up with 'secondary cognitive elaboration' – with the process of assimilat-

17. Austin (1971), Holmes (1973).
18. Holmes (1973) reports that, for convergers, 20 per cent of the rapid eye movement (REM) phase of sleep is taken up with bursts of sustained eye movement – the equivalent figure for divergers being only 11 per cent. Con-versely, convergers spend only 24 per cent of the REM phase with their eyes still, whereas divergers spend as much as 38 per cent.

ing those images into sensible-seeming patterns.[19] In other words, it seems to be the vivid visual images that the convergers fail to recall, whereas the more rational thoughts that follow these they recall perfectly well.

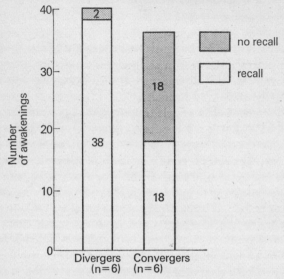

Figure 13. Dream recall by divergers and convergers when woken during rapid eye movement sleep

Freud claimed that those who repress fiercely will have poor access to 'primary process' thought: the stream of mental associations that authorities as diverse as Galton and Einstein have seen as essential to imaginative thought. Freud also claimed, quite specifically, that they will have poor access to their dreams. These present studies lend strong support to the view, then, that convergers are more likely than divergers to repress the non-rational aspects of their experience.[20]

19. Molinari and Foulkes (1969), Holmes (1973). Holmes shows that the two sorts of dream report are quite dissimilar in character. He also ensures that the differences observed between convergers and divergers cannot be explained away in terms either of their educational background or of their verbal fluency.
20. An analogous argument has been put forward by Witkin and his colleagues; Goodenough (1973). As one might expect, first-born sons tend to be convergers; McGuire (1974). First-borns also seem to be worse at recalling their dreams; Ward (1973).

Before hazarding a more formal interpretation, another body of evidence is worth examining. This harks back, again, to Chapter 6; but this time to the evidence about the images associated with the ideal types of the 'artist' and the 'scientist' – the first of whom is seen as warm, soft and exciting, while the second is seen as cold, hard and valuable. There is a curious feature about these stereotyped images: the age at which they crystallize or gel. For they take shape in our minds at different stages in our development; the image of the 'scientist' before we reach puberty, and that of the 'artist' during the course of adolescence itself.[21]

Some of these changes with age are set out in Figure 14; and in looking at these, it is important to grasp just how powerful such consensuses can become. The boys taking the test were faced with ten pairs of adjectives – like 'warm/cold', 'imaginative/unimaginative', 'hard/soft' – each arranged on a seven-point scale from 'extremely warm' for example, to 'extremely cold'. 100 per cent stereotyping would result if all the boys taking the test agreed in ascribing the same ten adjectives to a given figure with the maximum possible degree of emphasis – a very strange state of affairs indeed.

But why should the image of what is hard, cold and valuable take shape before adolescence, while that of what is warm, soft and exciting takes shape during it? Vico said of such images, we may recall, that they were the fruits of unreflective intelligence. Why, though, should one stereotyped image rather than another grip the unreflective intelligence of a whole age-group?

It seems that we stereotype our imagery most powerfully when this reflects issues of pressing concern to us. In psychological jargon, the stereotyping of images increases with the 'salience' of the images. Take an example. Between the ages of thirteen and seventeen academically gifted children are starting to separate themselves from their parents and immerse themselves in the world of their school. Accordingly, between the ages of thirteen and seventeen the images of Good Father and Good Mother – about whom, initially, there is massive consensus – begin to fragment. While at thirteen, almost all children are agreed that the Good Father and Good Mother are extremely warm,

21. Hudson (1968). Sample sizes in this kind of study are often large. In this instance, 390.

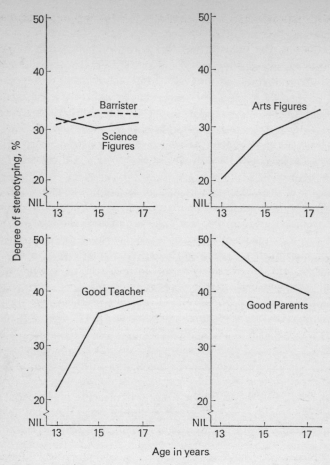

Figure 14. Changes in image with age

imaginative, intelligent and valuable, by seventeen this consensus has begun to break down. Adjectives are ascribed more cautiously; and differences between individuals in their choice of adjectives become more pronounced. However, while the consensus about parent figures is breaking down in this way, one about the Good Teacher is taking clear shape. By the age of seventeen the image of Good Father, Good Mother and Good Teacher are all etched with approximately equal clarity, parents having grown less important, teachers more so.[22]

During the same period, the consensus about figures like Mathematician, Physicist, Engineer and Biologist shifts scarcely at all; while those about Poet, Artist, Novelist and Historian – like the Good Teacher – sharpen progressively. An important figure in this context is the Lawyer, for, in the British Isles, he is broadly associated with the arts rather than with science; but is clearly an agent of lawfulness, authority and control, rather than of self-expression. The legal figure used in my study was the Barrister; and his image follows almost exactly the same path as the Scientist's – firmly established by thirteen, and thereafter changing scarcely at all.

Before leaving it, there is a last twist to this work on stereo-typed perception to be looked at, and it centres on the person's perception of himself. In another study of mine, I asked students to describe themselves in terms of the familiar categories; and found that young specialists in the humanities tended to see themselves as imaginative, warm and exciting, while the young physical science specialists saw themselves as valuable, dependable, intelligent and manly.[23] So much, you would expect. But there is more to the data than this. I asked each individual to make the judgments about himself in terms of four 'selves':

Actual Self (who he actually was).
Ideal Self (who he would like to be).
Perceived Self (who his teachers took him to be).
Future Self (who he expected to be in, say, ten years' time).

Now the self-images of the two groups of specialists differed more sharply using some of these 'selves' than others. And these differences fell into a neat pattern. It was simply this: that the differences involving the 'artistic' virtues (imaginative, warm

22. Confirmation of the view that stereotyping of perception increases with salience comes from an intimate study by Sheldrake and Turner (1973) of ideological conflict between two factions of staff members attached to a therapeutic community. The faction exercising control of the community held a more traditional, 'liberal' attitude towards psychiatry; the under-dog faction adopted the more radical posture associated with Szasz (1962a) and Laing (1967). It was members of the beleaguered radical faction who showed the greater simplicity and stereotyping in their judgments about the political conflict in which they were caught up.
23. Hudson (1968).

and exciting) were sharpest if one looked at Actual Self; while those involving the 'scientific' ones (valuable, dependable, and manly) were sharpest if one looked at Perceived Self. In other words, it was Actual Self that enabled these young men to be dispassionate about their possession of virtues associated with the arts, and Perceived Self about their possession of virtues associated with science. 'Artistic' virtues, it seems, are perceived by internal reference, by looking inside oneself; whereas the 'scientific' ones are perceived by reference to figures in authority like the teacher. And this fits neatly with the view that the image of the artist is essentially libidinous. It is a symbolic representation of pleasurable impulses that we see as internal to ourselves. While the image of the scientist symbolizes the sense of rectitude – the 'super ego' that we acquire from the powerful figures around us.[24] This distinction between the pleasurable impulse that wells up from inside and the conscience that is imposed from outside, has a bearing on the 'fixation hypothesis' I want to expound next.

24. Technically, this process is known as 'introjection'.

10 Ways of Life

The time has now come to stitch these various items of information together. In doing this, I shall shift somewhat from the field of evidence to that of interpretation, which is at times necessarily speculative. For all broad schematic statements about human needs lie beyond the range of evidence that we now know how to collect. The example offered here is put forward because it is compact, and because it helps to make explicit certain beliefs that have been influential in the shaping of my own research.

Attempts to draw up lists of human needs have in the past proved a disappointment, being either too simple to be credible, or so diffuse as to lose their explanatory leverage. Most authorities now concede that any grand lexicon of human needs is out of place. But simple formulations are difficult too. It has recently been proposed, for instance, that human beings are primarily moved by a single urge: that to reduce uncertainty – to know. But no sooner has a persuasive idea of this kind been put forward than it is drowned out with exceptions. And with alternatives, too. For we can just as sensibly say of adults that, at root, they are motivated by the need for respect; or, for that matter, by anxiety.

I want now to present a scheme that contrasts two levels of need: 'primitive energy' and 'symbolic preoccupation'. At the primitive level, this acknowledges the existence of a variety of needs – sex, aggression, jealousy, competitiveness, the need to belong, and so on – but is concerned with the distinction between two categories of impulse: the pleasure-seeking and the destructive. It also postulates that these primitive impulses can be translated or transformed: turned, that is to say, from a desire for physical action, into a desire for activity that is symbolic. When transformed (or 'sublimated') in this way, pleasure-seeking energy becomes a desire for exploration and discovery; while destructive energy becomes a desire for orderliness and control.[1] A need for symbolic exploration is expressed as a need to probe the non-rational, forbidden or strange. A concern for symbolic control is expressed as a desire to avoid ambiguity, to be right, and to be in the right. The transformation of pleasure-seeking energies leads to transgression or dissolution of boundaries; the transformation of the destructive ones to their maintenance and fortification. The first leads to what Norman O. Brown has called an 'erotic' sense of reality; the second to an 'aggressive' one – a need to bend the world to one's own will.

These ideas are really ones about the *transformation* of impulse. Their implication is that the individual shifts to the symbolic level of expression when he finds expression at the physical level impracticable. They assume that, in the civilized state, the expression of a primitive impulse generates anxiety or guilt; and that it is this which, in its turn, 'fuels' the transformation to the symbolic level.

As stated, the scheme is of course clumsy. We know that motives are characteristically mixed. Also, as the vicious circle in Chapter 5 implies, that the transformation of need is by no means always in an 'upwards' direction. Frustration may cause a 'lateral' transposition – a shift from one symbolic need to another. Or, if more comprehensive, it may lead to a transformation that is 'regressive'; and in which a desire, say, for symbolic control is replaced by one for physical aggression. But, for the moment, let the scheme stand as it is; its better points will become a little clearer in the next page or two.

For the present purpose, the years of human growth are divided into three blocks: infancy, childhood, and adolescence. The points of transition between these vary, of course, from individual to individual and from culture to culture. But in our own society a number of major changes certainly confront each child somewhere between the ages of five and seven. He begins his formal education. He passes, the child psychologists tell us, from the 'Oedipal phase', in which he is taken up with relationships within the family, and enters what classical psychoanalytic theory calls the 'latency period'.[2] This is seen as a phase of six

1. The notion of energy transformation throws many psychologists into a panic. Yet we must choose. Either we admit some such principle, or we postulate an absurd array of sophisticated needs, all 'wired in' at birth.
2. 'Latency' is a term out of fashion, but useful all the same.

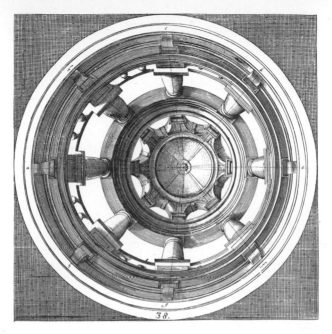

The architectural metaphor of the self (from Jan Vredeman de Vries's *Perspective*, 1604, reproduced from Dover Publications' edition of 1968)

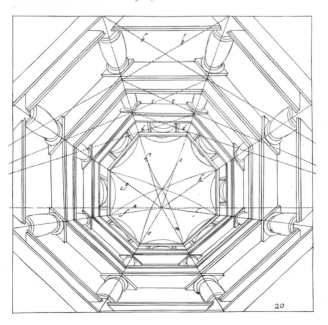

Peter's drawings

3

4

7

8

11

12

15

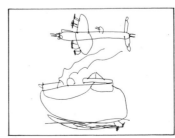

16

Above Wera Knoop, the inspiration of Rilke's *Sonnets to Orpheus* (reproduced by kind permission of the heirs of Rainer Maria Rilke and Insel Verlag)

Opposite 'A Pioneer tells the truth and treasures the honor of his unit' (from *Two Worlds of Childhood : U.S. and U.S.S.R.* by Urie Bronfenbrenner, reproduced by kind permission of George Allen & Unwin)

р ПАВЛИК МОРОЗОВ

ПИОНЕР
ГОВОРИТ
ПРАВДУ,
ОН ДОРОЖИТ
ЧЕСТЬЮ
СВОЕГО ОТРЯДА.

'Bather' (1925) by Pierre Bonnard (© by A.D.A.G.P. Paris, 1974)

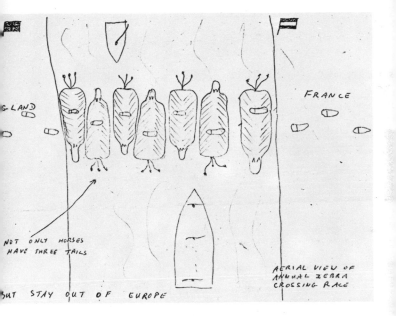

'Every year there is a race from England to France. Every zoo in the country rounds up its zebras and drives them into the English Channel to form a sort of bridge. Then the handlers walk over the Channel by stepping from zebra to zebra. On the return journey the zebras walk over the men, and who can blame them . . .' Aerial view of annual zebra crossing race

Charlie Parker (photograph by Tony Williams from *Bird Lives!*
by Ross Russell, reproduced by kind permission of Tony Williams
and Quartet Books Ltd)

or seven years, between infancy and adolescence, when emotional, sexual preoccupations are to some extent dormant. At the age of seven or eight, the child also passes – the Swiss developmental psychologist Jean Piaget suggests – from one moral stage to another: initially, his sense of morality is authoritarian and absolute, but sometime during his primary education, this changes to an attitude which is more realistic and humane.[3]

His first years at school are ones in which the child must subjugate his 'impulse life' in order to concentrate on the impersonal skills of reading, writing and arithmetic. It is also a time when, at least initially, he thinks in terms of unusually rigid moral categories, distinguishing in a black-and-white way between right and wrong. A different crisis awaits him at the onset of puberty. There, the massive hormonal changes that herald sexual maturity throw him back once more upon his earlier preoccupations with life's personal, erotic possibilities.

The evidence about the imagery surrounding the arts and sciences now plays its part. For the images that crystallize during latency (those of the scientist and barrister) are those that caricature the dominant pre-occupations of that phase: the righteous subjugation of impulse in the service of impersonal, objective skill. Likewise, the stereotyped image that crystallizes *during* adolescence – that of the artist – is one that parodies the predominant issues of *that* age too: the conflict of intensely personal desires and sensitivities with the puritanical system of values already established.

The 'fixation hypothesis' amounts to this simple assertion: that a person's frame of mind takes on its enduring shape during one of these three stages – infancy, latency, adolescence; and that each stage of fixation is associated with its own characteristic way of life. Simple-seeming, the hypothesis carries implications about the nature of the individual's habits of thought; and, with a little tinkering, it tells us something about existential matters too.

The individual who fixates in infancy, is someone whom the incest taboo has failed to expel. Psychically, he remains trapped within the family. He will think intuitively. Also, because he fixates before he has any objectifying skills – before he can read and write – he is someone, we predict, who will prove incapable

3. Piaget (1932).

of crisp discriminations between facts and wishes, between the rational and non-rational, between the 'I' and the 'not-I', between people and things. His fortifications are permeable. In the jargon, he has weak 'ego-boundaries'; and, hence, good access to his own 'primary process' thought.

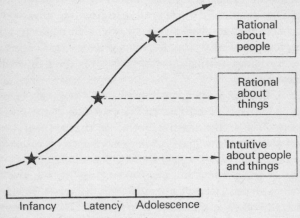

Figure 15. The fixation hypothesis

The person who fixates during the latency period offers a total contrast. For whatever reason, he has been vigorously expelled from the Oedipal nexus, and feels an unusually pressing need to establish for himself a secure position outside it. He thinks in an orderly, analytic way; he likes to be rule-bound; and is happiest dealing with the world of things. His ego-boundaries will be rigidly defined; and he will distinguish sharply between the objective truth and his own wishes. And – a delicate point – whereas the fixator-in-infancy will see as real only his own inner life, the fixator-in-latency will see as real only what is *external*. His sense of reality is based squarely in the concrete world outside. He needs to be in the right; and his equilibrium, his sanity even, depends on a sense of order.

The life of the fixator-in-adolescence is a more complicated affair. For, when he comes to fixate, he already possesses quite high levels of conceptual skill. In returning to the world of emotion, he cannot plunge back, neck and crop, as though he were an infant, into the world of intimate relations. Instead, he must achieve a compromise; and the compromise lies in the use of rational systems of thought upon subject-matter that is inherently personal. He tries to be objective about the subjective; to treat the personal impersonally. Expelled from the nuclear family, he is held to it by a long, elastic thread. And although his ego-boundaries are strong, as with the fixator-in-latency, he is compelled continually to reach across these boundaries, and attempt to colonize the irrational world outside. His mode of address is that of symbolic exploration. He needs to tempt danger, to prize up the lid of Pandora's box – to tease out and objectify human feelings, and the potentialities of human relationships.

As stated, the fixation hypothesis is not just highly speculative; it is also too pat. The types it generates are caricatures; and it takes no adequate account of differences in style that we know exist – the 'mixed' type, for instance, whose interest is in people, but who wants to gain administrative control over them, rather than to learn about them. Instead of elaborating the model to account for such distinctions, I would prefer to make explicit the metaphor that underlies it; and then to show how it makes sense of some further evidence about the ways of life people actually lead.[4]

For the metaphor that lurks beneath the fixation hypothesis is the one we have already met in Chapter 4 in the context of the octagons: the idea of a defensive wall or fortification. Patently, it is drawn from military architecture; and it encourages us to see the fixator-in-latency as though he were a medieval fortified town, with massive defensive walls and controlled access by means of drawbridge and portcullis. The fixator-in-adolescence is seen more as a modern urban sprawl; while the fixator-in-infancy, on this argument, is more a nomadic encampment, with virtually no architectural organization at all.

Granted that this metaphor possesses some validity, the essential distinctions between the three fixators lie, then, in their relation to what is alien or strange. Threatened by what is alien, the fixator-in-infancy simply moves camp; he shifts from one pitch to another, carrying his own internal domestic arrangements with him. In contrast, the fixator-in-latency stands or falls

4. Many people experience an overwhelming compulsion to read judgments of value into any comparison one makes between early and late fixators – (or between convergers and divergers). I can only say that none is intended.

by the robustness of his fortified walls. He may make sallies into the surrounding countryside, subjugating local savages to the rule of reason; and he beats off intruders with slings, arrows and boiling oil. Either he is sovereign, or he allies himself to someone else's sovereignty – if he does neither, he is deposed. The fixator-in-adolescence, by the very nature of his architectural arrangements, must assimilate the alien by means that are less forthright. He colonizes the surrounding countryside less by force of arms than by discretionary trade agreements; and he assimilates the alien intruder not by blunt confrontation, but by guerilla tactics and surreptitious collaboration. The alien is not eluded, nor slain at the boundary wall, but assimilated and – more or less effectively – defused.[5]

The evidence we possess about early, middling and late-fixators is abundant – although rather lop-sided, largely dealing with the fixator-in-latency, the physical scientist. In a brilliant speculative essay published a decade ago, David McClelland reviewed a great deal of this evidence about scientists, and argued that the key to their personalities lay in the difficulty they experienced in coping with aggression.[6] Their work, subjugating the external world to impersonal laws, is thus the symbolic expression of a destructiveness that might otherwise be vented – quite uncontrollably – on people.

In marshalling the evidence, McClelland stressed the following points:

1. Experimental physical scientists come from Puritan backgrounds, although not themselves religious. Historically, modern science has developed in close association with Puritanism; and as Robert Merton has said, there is a 'point-to-point' correlation between 'the principles of Puritanism and the attributes, goals and results of science'.

5. I have said nothing here about the causes of early or late fixation. There seems little point at this stage in laying one essentially speculative discussion on top of another. My guess, for what it is worth, is that a vital part of the causal sequence will be found to lie in the 'sexual organization' of the family. There is no reason, though, why such fundamental aspects of the individual's specification should not be established very early in life, even in the womb. For an introduction to recent studies of early interactions between mother and child, see Richards (1974).
6. McClelland (1970).

2. Science is a sphere dominated by men; and scientists themselves are intensely 'masculine' – they are 'male', that is to say, in their sense of their own gender, in their interests, and in the social ambience they create.

3. Although scientists work together in teams, create professional institutions and work towards institutional rewards, they avoid intimate personal contact – and in particular, personal aggression. In McClelland's phrase, 'scientists react emotionally to human emotions and try to avoid them'. It is not so much that the scientist withdraws from human contacts; rather – as Silverman has claimed – that 'he is simply limiting these to some small number of a particular type which he feels able to deal with'.[7]

4. Physical scientists like music and photography, but dislike painting and poetry. They like impersonal representation; they dislike the personal or allusive.

5. From an early age, they develop a strong interest in the structure of the material world. Physical scientists typically develop a strong interest in the structure of the natural world 'between the ages of five and ten': one that is 'easily recognized as dominant by the boys themselves, by their teachers, and by their parents'.

6. Scientists who are creative are usually hard-working to the extent of appearing obsessed.

As a profession, we have in the past tended to see as 'mature', 'integrated', 'well-adjusted' and 'creative' those patterns of behaviour that most strongly resemble our own. The scientist, as he emerges from McClelland's review, we are inclined to view as a man mildly estranged from his true nature: even as mildly pathological. A life bereft of 'rich personal relations' is, we imply, scarcely a life at all.

Very slowly, we are learning to see the strengths of modes of adaptation that are unlike ours; and the weaknesses of our own. And we are doing so, again, in terms of evidence that is surpris-

7. Himself a physical scientist, Silverman (in press) ascribes this deliberate restriction to a 'failure in the sense of human connectedness with the mother in the early years'.

ingly specific. The key to the thinking that we are now trying to do in this slippery zone lies, as before, in the idea of impulse shaped and contained by conventionally defined boundary states.[8] The proposition underlying this research is quite simple: that in the course of any specialized education or training, we acquire not only specific mental skills and a discipline, but a way of life. These ways of life are, at least in part, the management of impulse writ large: projections on to the screen of public life of processes that we each endure more privately. The conventions that bound these ways of life – like the images of the arts and sciences – are part of the 'deep' or hidden structure of what our education transmits. The life we lead is one that centres, to a considerable extent, around the observance or transgression of these bounding conventions.

The studies of life-style I want to mention are all severely factual. They deal with people whose intellectual training has been highly specialized and whose thinking has reached a very marked degree of focus. They concern people in bulk – which proves an irritating limitation – and, initially, deal only with the barest bones of a life-style: the information on births, deaths, marriages and divorces that public sources contain.

In the first of these pieces of work, Bernadine Jacot and I looked at the details of the personal lives of eminent British academics appearing in *Who's Who*.[9] Specialists in the humanities, the biological sciences, and the physical sciences, we found, each had their characteristic pattern. In the humanities, rates of marriage were low, and likewise those of fertility. Among the distinguished scholars in the classics, for example, fully 41 per cent were without children, as compared with 8 per cent among biologists. Almost all eminent biologists, in contrast, married; and many had large families. On the other hand, their rates of divorce were, for their generation, surprisingly high. Eminent physical scientists were only a little less likely than the biologists

8. A thought to brood upon: the Victorians saw as 'manly' and 'virile' the man who scrupulously contained his sexual impulses, and as 'effeminate' the man who indulged them. In other words, they equated masculinity with a strong boundary wall, and effeminacy with a weak or permeable one. McClelland's scientists are close to this masculine ideal: manly in their interests, style and self-image, but with their impulse lives under careful control.

9. Hudson and Jacot (1971).

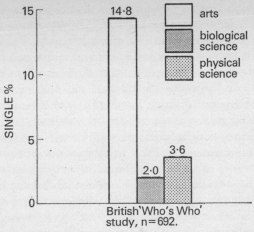

Figure 16. The proportion of humanists, biologists and physical scientists who remain single

to marry; they had rather fewer children, however, and were *un*likely to divorce.

Looking back to the fixation hypothesis, we see that the broad arts/science difference in rates of marriage (and hence fertility) fit comfortably into place. According to the hypothesis, the choice of human subject-matter is linked to a freedom from social convention. Specialists in the humanities may be less likely to marry than scientists because, being more interested in personal intimacy, they are more alert to its hazards and ambiguities as well as its rewards. But they may also be less likely to marry because they find it natural to transgress conventional boundaries; in particular, those conventions and boundaries that define the masculine sex role. They are more likely to acknowledge to themselves that they are in some degree effeminate or homosexual; less likely to marry simply because it is conventional to do so. A similar pattern of results has emerged from a recent survey of American university teachers: on both sides of the Atlantic, and over a substantial period of time, there would seem to be a connection between the humanities and the avoidance of the married state.[10] In contrast, the attitude of the scientist to marriage seems to be both more conventional and more perfunctory.

10. Hudson (1973a).

But what about the biologists, and divorce? Our hypothesis ought to cover this, and it does not. Interpretatively, the evidence requires some care. The broad distinction between the arts and sciences is a dangerously crude one, lumping together groups of people we know to be quite dissimilar. To take three instances, we know that the physical and biological sciences recruit students of different intellectual types (the first being substantially more convergent than the second).[11] Also that among the physical scientists, there are pronounced differences between physicists and chemists. Students at Cambridge reading physics usually have a heavy bias towards non-verbal reasoning, whereas those in chemistry show a more even balance between the verbal and the non-verbal.[12] And among physicists, there are differences between experimentalists and theoreticians: Anne Roe reports that distinguished experimentalists appear to reason in terms of visual images while their theoretical colleagues think in terms of numerical symbols.[13]

The point, interpretatively speaking, is that we should *expect* our broader categories to break down; and we should *expect*, sooner or later, to have to examine the finer grain. Returning to the divorce statistics, we find sizeable differences, subject by subject, generation by generation, social class by social class. The *Who's Who* physicists are six times as likely to divorce as are the chemists. Rates also differed widely among the eminent biologists; these are high among those from private schools, low among those from state schools; and – more surprisingly – higher among those born in the first decade of the century, lower among those born in the second. One looks for simple sociological or demographic explanations, but none fits. What *is* clear though – when you look at the names – is that the biologists with the highest divorce rates are those who helped to set experimental biology on its feet as a discipline.

And this is the interpretative thread we need. Divorce-prone biologists are those who rise to eminence during a revolutionary phase in their discipline's growth. An ability to breach the walls of convention in the intellectual sphere is associated, in other words, with the propensity to breach them in the personal sphere

11. Hudson (1966).
12. Hudson (1960).
13. Roe (1953).

as well. Other evidence from the *Who's Who* study tends to support this. Among philosophers, for instance, such divorces as there are cluster among those born in the second decade of the century, not the first: among those who ushered in the positivistic revolution in Oxford philosophy rather than among the neo-Hegelians they deposed.

Perhaps most telling of all in this respect, because it brought out clearly the association with social class, was a small but detailed study of our own in Edinburgh, based on the marriages of young research students.[14] We found that while there were differences between the marriages of those in the arts and sciences, the most obvious differences were those between two groups of biologists. These two groups were picked solely in terms of the husband's work: on the one hand, the more traditional biologists – physiologists, zoologists, animal behaviourists – and on the other the 'physical' biologists – the geneticists and biochemists who bring to the study of animate subject-matter the techniques and assumptions of mathematics and physical science.

The first group came from middle-class homes, and had highly educated wives, with whom they conducted egalitarian but what seemed to be somewhat de-sexualized lives – lives, that is to say, in which sex, and the differences between the sexes, played little part. The second came from more working-class homes. They had married girls who were conspicuously less educated than themselves, and who were content to fill the traditional wifely role.

There are details about these two groups of wives that struck us as particularly revealing. Almost without exception those married to the traditional biologists, and whose marriages were egalitarian, came to interviews somewhat carelessly dressed; whereas those married to the physical biologists were evidently clothes-conscious, and came smartly dressed. Also, almost without exception, those in the first group were girls who had first menstruated rather late (after the age of fourteen), whereas those in the second had menstruated early. And this difference is significant because of what we know about early and late maturers. Kinsey claims that the sexual differences between the

14. Hudson, Johnston and Jacot (1972); Hudson, Jacot and Sheldrake (1973).

two are important only at extremes.[15] On the other hand, Hamburg and Lunde point to evidence that early maturers are more socially 'submissive' – and more submissive, presumably, in adopting the traditional wifely role.[16] There seems to exist, in other words, a close relation between the husband's line of attack in purely academic matters; his social class of origin; the level of education of the girl he marries; her personality; and the extent to which they pursue a conventionally sexualized relationship or a more egalitarian and de-sexualized one.

Evidently, the connections between social class, styles of marriage, and the husband's choice of work are worth pursuing. We know, on the basis of both American and British research, that couples from working-class backgrounds are more likely than those from the middle class to adopt a conventional segregation into male and female roles. We also suspect on the basis of the *Who's Who* evidence, that – in a hierarchically organized society like the British Isles – radical innovations in intellectual life are made either by 'outsiders' (Australians, New Zealanders, South Africans, Americans, Canadians, European emigrés), or by mavericks from privileged homes.[17]

If new fields of research are set in being by 'outsiders', and by the unconventional products of privileged homes, work of the second wave – often brilliant, but 'safer' – will be done by people who are more conventional but less privileged. Thus the kinds of experimental biology that were on the very brink of scientific awareness fifty years ago are now part of its fashionable mainstream: once a territory for mavericks, this variety of research is now an academic thoroughfare for the more conventionally ambitious. The kind of person who contributes early on may be quite different, psychologically speaking, from the kind who contributes later.

By now this web of evidence and interpretation has spread out considerably. Beginning with what we know about the physical basis of our activating desires, and the relatively simple-seeming question of our sexual identity, we have moved into the al-

15. Kinsey (1953).
16. Hamburg and Lunde (1967).
17. Among other reasons, because working-class mavericks have frequently been forced to leave school early and earn a living. But also perhaps because, as the trans-sexual writer James Morris says, 'the whole of English upper-class life' is 'shot through with bisexual instinct'.

together more complex issues of the individual's habitual frame of mind and way of life. How these various aspects of each person's biography fit together we do not yet quite see; and while the fixation hypothesis suggests an integration, this remains a model, a heuristic device – a way of looking for understanding rather than understanding itself. This said, though, progress has been made, and the sense is strong of more to follow. Seen through the hungry eyes of a research worker looking for his next project, the field adumbrated in the last three chapters positively teems with possibilities. Prospectors in a richly workable terrain, we have not yet staked out the landscape into lots. But – there is no doubt about it – the description of these quite fundamental aspects of everyday experience is now launched, and what has been achieved so far will soon seem no more than a beginning.

Part Four

Life Before Death

11   The Idea of Freedom

Helpful though it is, the kind of factual evidence about our personal lives deployed in the last three chapters often seems a little clumsy. It deals with aspects of our personal experience that concern us closely, but does so in ways that are slightly wooden. And this woodenness reflects more than the sheer difficulty of collecting and organizing data: it echoes the philosophical assumptions that such factual research seems inevitably to tow in its wake. If it is hard to collect systematic information about the aspects of our lives that matter to us most, it is ten times harder to do so in ways that will not distort what we seek to describe.

We are back, in other words, frustratingly close to where we began: with the spectre of the psychologist shadow-boxing with his subject-matter, creating castles of facts and over-simplified theories – theories that bear on the lives we actually lead only in the manner of an identikit or tailor's dummy. The contours are there, we feel; all the outward signs. But the sense of the fabric itself, its real stuff and substance, is missing.

It is this sense of immediacy – the novelist's greatest advantage over the psychologist – that we abandon the moment we are committed to the paraphernalia of statistical argument or to the systematic exploration of theory. The loss is dangerous. For technical argument can disguise alien ideological assumptions; and it can also embody them. Psychological research, among much else, is an expression of beliefs about what people are really like; and when these beliefs gain a cultural foothold, to this extent they alter our view of what people are. The academic psychologist is thus engaged in psychic engineering; in the alteration of human self-awareness. The engineering done so far has centred on the idea of freedom, and there are serious questions about whether this had been adroit. But before we look at

the engineering itself, there exists a nest of muddles and misconceptions that psychologists have woven round the philosophical problems of determinism and free will. These we must clear
up first.

Running through my comments, the reader will find a sustained hostility towards the naïve physical determinism that has
been the dominant view of human beings held by scientifically
minded psychologists for the last fifty years. This is the doctrine
colloquially known as 'materialism'. It holds that physical
events are 'real', whereas mental ones are not; that physical laws
govern human beings, in ways that make ideas of freedom and
personal responsibility illusory; and that human beings' behaviour should, in their own interests, be brought under
scientific control. Naïve physical determinism is the philosophy
that sustains us all from time to time, and sustains the behaviourists continuously. At its heart is the belief that 'in the last
analysis' and 'when the chips are down' people are bodies, and
bodies are things.

Behaviourism, although a psychological doctrine, is clearly
related to two doctrines from philosophy: materialism and positivism. Materialism is a system of metaphysical beliefs, centring
on the idea that matter is the primary stuff of the universe.
Logical positivism is a theory of knowledge, which claims that
all metaphysical ideas are meaningless – materialistic ones included. Strictly speaking, you cannot be both a materialist and a
positivist. Nevertheless, behaviourists often back both these far-
fetched systems of belief at the same time. Historically, there
also exists a powerful link between materialism, as a philosophy
and as a way of life, and puritanism.

One of the central oddities of this link between systems of
ideas is that those who profess materialism most energetically
seem to be those cut off most conclusively from a life of sensual
pleasure – from a delight in the material world itself. Professor
Skinner's Utopia, Walden Two, is a place of polite recreations –
and this would seem symptomatic of a more diffuse unease, in
the United States especially, about forthright physical enjoyment.[1] The person who asserts the primacy of material things
appears the last among men to enjoy a good meal, a night with

1. Skinner (1948).

his wife or mistress, or simply a walk in the fresh air. Conversely, it is the Catholic French whose serious concern with food and drink, sex and the sophistications of women's clothes reflects a more direct appreciation of what the material world has to offer. Paradoxically, then, materialism is an ascetic view of life – but half-heartedly ascetic, because those in its grip feel compelled to try to enjoy those material possessions they accumulate. They feel compelled to try, but their pleasure never quite rings true.

The classical statement of the connection between puritanism and the spirit of capitalism is Max Weber's; and his model has been extended by McClelland to encompass the part played in the maintenance of this connection by patterns of child-raising.[2] There remains a good deal of sorting out to do, even so. We may hypothesize that puritan religion fuels (or in some more subtle way legitimates) commercial growth; that commercial growth leads to the growth of technology; and that it is the technology of the automobile, the central-heating plant and the television that insulates us systematically from the direct enjoyment of our own natures. I would also wish to argue, though, that materialism flows from puritanical religion more directly than this, because it is sensual pleasure that the puritan wishes to attack – and sensual pleasure, although *about* the physical, resides in the mind.

Thus our view of human nature must accommodate the gratifications of the flesh or be treated as mistaken. Certainly I would not take seriously any doctrine that led to the polite desiccation of Walden Two. Equally, however, it is a mistake to assume – as the puritans themselves appear to – that such gratifications are a simple matter; that they are something we achieve by being spontaneous. I shall argue, on the contrary, that the human biography takes shape under conditions of continual and unresolvable tension between the forces of self-expression and those of control; between the desire for spontaneous utterance and the necessities of disciplinary constraint. The nature of this tension is examined, in this chapter, in terms of the idea of freedom, and of the influence of that idea on the upbringing and education children receive. It is, if you like, a dialogue between Eros and Thanatos – on the one hand, the need to express, relate

2. Weber (1930), McClelland (1961); also Skinner (1974b).

and explore; and on the other, to control and restrain. This dialogue has subtle reverberations. It influences the extent to which we can encompass both pleasure and shame within the bounds of a single relationship. It also governs, in very considerable detail, the nature of creative work.[3]

Freud and a behaviourist like Watson differed in many things; but in one respect, they stood on common ground. When thinking about psychology, both were determinists. Freud believed that his discoveries about the unconscious had absolved man from the Victorian disease of guilt and had scotched Victorian preoccupations with will-power. Where Copernicus had removed man from the centre of the universe, and Darwin had removed from him his status as a creature especially created by God, Freud saw himself as completing the process of demystification. Man, he claimed, in his *General Introduction to Psychoanalysis*, was a creature 'lived by the unconscious'.[4] 'The deeply rooted belief in psychic freedom and choice ... is quite unscientific and must give ground before the claims of a determinism which governs mental life.'

Just as there were evolutionists before Darwin, there were men before Freud who were both determinists and believers in the primacy of the unconscious. The eighteenth-century Scottish philosopher David Hume claimed that 'reason is, and ought only to be, the slave of the passions'. Wilhelm Wundt, one of the founding fathers of experimental psychology, observed, whilst Freud was still a child, that 'the unconscious mind is for us like an unknown being who creates and produces for us, and finally throws the ripe fruits in our lap'. As Lancelot Whyte puts it, the topic of the unconscious was 'conceivable' in 1700, 'topical' in 1800, and by 1900 'positively fashionable'.[5]

Freud was neither the first, then, nor alone. His achievement lay in establishing a memorable language or rhetoric, in which current assumptions about the unconscious could be treated as

3. Marxist argument follows this dialectical pattern; but by no means all dialectical argument is Marxist. In any case, Marxists frequently assume that the dialectic can be resolved in some Utopian condition; whereas the tensions that concern the psychologist are those that in principle are unresolvable – and remain potentially productive for that very reason.
4. Freud (1938), cited by May (1969).
5. Whyte (1962) – a salutary antidote to the belief that ideas of the unconscious sprang from Freud's brow fully-formed.

though they were scientific truths. When a behaviourist speaks about the laws of conditioning, he offers an alternative language, a rival rhetoric. Though many of their more detailed assumptions differ, both rhetorics spring from the same deterministic core. They assert the existence of a 'block universe', in which each event is fully, causally controlled; a universe in which there are no gaps, and in which each of us does what the forces of heredity and environment require.

It is not for psychologists to resolve perennial philosophical problems, but over the matter of determinism and free will, we seem to have become quite addled. The Victorians took the wrong turning, Freud among them; and, like sheep, we have trooped passively in their train.

At root, the argument is simple. Obviously, the psychologist must believe that what he is looking at is lawful. (His only alternative is to believe that people are arbitrary or random – which in certain respects they may be. But there is no comfort in that.[6]) He must also believe that some of the causal processes that act on a person are internal to that person: that men have heads, and that important things take place inside them. And unless he is a helpless bigot, he must believe, too, that some of these internal causes take the form of ideas: that we are influenced by what we know, what we believe and what we assume.

People differ; and what matters as far as arguments about determinism and free will go is that they differ in terms of the relationship they envisage between themselves and the world about them. Some see themselves as agents and initiators: people who can shape their own lives, influence other people, get things done. Others see themselves as cogs in a machine. Others see themselves as helpless victims – pawns of forces that lie outside themselves. And people who see themselves as agents – who assume they can plan and initiate, and that they are responsible for what they do – act in ways that differ from those who see themselves as cogs or victims.

Where, then, is our problem? It lies in our stubborn impulse to say, as Freud said, 'Ah, but that so-called agent's sense of his own freedom is *illusory*.' This is the crux of the matter, for this

6. Monod (1972) has stressed the randomness of basic physical processes: this of course has no bearing on whether complex human action is random. The two issues are distinct.

reaction is ambiguous. It consists of two separate propositions rolled into one. The first is a platitude; the second is a mistake.

The statement implies, in the first place, that the agent's sense of freedom is governed by causes over which, ultimately, he has no control. As an assertion of faith, this is harmless; it commits us to nothing. However, the second implication is altogether more arbitrary. It holds that a person's sense of agency is itself of no practical, causal significance; that it is immaterial whether someone sees himself as a victim, an agent or a cog – his behaviour will be the same in all three cases. There exists, as far as I know, no evidence to support this startling claim; and a great deal at the level of common-sense observation to suggest that it is false. Whatever our capacity, we know that the agents among the people we deal with behave differently from the victims: they undertake more, and, because they impose themselves on events, frequently leave behind something new, with the stamp of their own personalities upon it. It is just this – the emergent sense of agency, of 'intentionality' – that the processes of upbringing and education should be concerned to foster.[7]

Interestingly enough, while Freud fell for this confusion between agents and cogs or victims in thinking about his patients, he avoided it in thinking about himself. Of himself he said: 'A man who has been the indisputable favourite of his mother keeps for life the feeling of a conqueror, that confidence of success that often induces real success.'[8]

Knowing where his conqueror's confidence came from in no way detracted from the confidence itself, nor should it have done. Quite the reverse. Far from weakening his self-confidence, Freud's ability to offer an explanation of it may well have strengthened his faith in its unshakeable reality. He was, after all, a prodigiously self-confident man.

That, as far as the philosophy of determinism goes, is all the psychologist needs to know.[9] Even so, such conceptual muddles

7. Shotter (1973) claims, in this context, that research on the behaviour of mothers with their infants is misconceived unless it is focused on the mother's concern for the 'intentional structure' taking shape in her child's mind. A sophisticated analysis of recent thinking about 'social meaning' and 'intention' is given by Quentin Skinner (1974).
8. Jones (1961), p. 6.
9. Some Anglo-Saxons have seen the resolution to the problems of free will and determinism in the writings of Jean-Paul Sartre. To my eye, his views are obscure. Also much more behaviouristic in tone than is sometimes

do not just happen. Psychologists are intelligent men and women, appearances sometimes to the contrary; and in the ordinary run of academic debate, confusions of this order would normally be sorted out quickly and permanently. Those surrounding the concepts of determinism and free will, however, crop up over and over again. No sooner do psychologists touch on a sensitive topic – race or the position of women – than the operation of reason ceases: professors become belligerent, and symbolic warfare begins.[10]

We confront here what Rollo May has called the 'endemic disease' of the twentieth century: a tendency to see ourselves as the passive product of a psychological and economic 'juggernaut'.[11] Increasingly, we have come to see ourselves as trapped: by psychological and economic forces, certainly; but trapped symbolically too – by the prospect of factual knowledge about how these supposedly inexorable psychological and economic forces work.

Whenever issues of liberty are at stake, furious debates ensue about evidence that is, in itself, highly technical: about statistical differences in I.Q. between racial groups, for example, or about the relation of the menstrual cycle to the moods of women. The quarrels which rage then consolidate around two debating positions, both of which are specious: on the one hand, the 'expert' who portrays himself as someone fearlessly telling the truth that others are too irrational to face; and on the other, the 'liberal', who believes that some scientific truths are too politically damaging to publish, and hence should be suppressed in the name of 'social responsibility'. What neither acknowledges is the logical irrelevance of such evidence to the political issue.

Take the uproar surrounding racial research on intelligence.[12] Grant, for the sake of argument, that black children turn out, on average, to be worse at intelligence tests than white children. This evidence is of the greatest significance as propaganda; but, logically, it is devoid of bearing on issues of educational or

---

imagined: 'It is not in some hiding-place that we will discover ourselves; it is on the road, in the town, in the midst of the crowd, a thing among things, a man among men.' Sartre (1970).

10. For a detailed account of one such case, see Hudson (1972).

11. May (1969).

12. For a naïve statement of this expert's position, see Jensen (1969). Critiques of this are offered in, for example, Richardson (1972).

political liberty. It can be used as ammunition, in justifying racial segregation, apartheid, the redirection of educational funds; but the inferences involved are farcically far-flung, and are acceptable only to someone whose mind is already closed.

We see this if we give all our cards away, and allow the racially preoccupied psychologist everything he wishes for. Grant that on every conceivable measure of intellectual excellence, black children turn out to be worse on average than whites.[13] Grant, too, that this difference can be shown conclusively to be genetic in origin – that the existence of racial prejudice merely confirms and consolidates what the genetic code dictates.[14] We are none the wiser as parents or teachers: we must still take each child on his merits, and do for him what we can. The colour of his skin, and the average ability of the racial group from which he springs, are irrelevant. Nor are we any the wiser as educational planners. Logically, the evidence does not justify placing children of different races into different streams, tracks or schools. Still less does it justify the redirection of educational funds from one racial group to another – or, for that matter, from one ability group to another, irrespective of race. The benefits to children of integrated schooling are a factual issue, but one that we must settle separately. Likewise, the benefits to society as a whole of spending more or less in any one educational sector. (It may well prove that, by the year 2000, we will have had to spend vastly more on the education of the urban poor, and will have decided to leave the better endowed to fend very largely for themselves.)

In taking such decisions, we ought to use evidence; but not the evidence that the race researchers press so eagerly upon us. Theirs looks vaguely 'important'. But it does so only as long as we remain in thrall to a particular form of the deterministic fallacy: the superstitions that if a human quality is inherited, it cannot be altered – whereas if it is caused by the environment, after birth, it can. Both are erroneous. Once again, ideology and fantasy have swamped out logic. Our body-build, we inherit; but what we make of that natural endowment, as office workers, athletes, or yogi, is very much a matter of training. Like Charles Atlas, we may begin as seven-stone weaklings, but end as

13. And irrespective of whether the tests are constructed by blacks or whites.
14. At present, we lack any technically convincing means of demonstrating this; but grant it, none the less.

mountains of rippling muscle. Conversely, many of the qualities that we acquire from our relations with others seem to be stamped into us, to all intents and purposes, irrevocably.

Inherited characteristics require an environment, a culture, within which to find expression; they are expressed, in other words, to greater or lesser degree depending upon the nature of that environment. The extent to which a given quality has been influenced by genetic factors, is one question; the extent to which that quality is modifiable in the light of further experience is another. We can assume no connection between them. Consequently, arguments in psychology about heredity *versus* environment are meaningless. And the more sophisticated versions of these arguments, which are couched in terms of 'heritability', and which slice up a quality like I.Q. into percentages – '80 per cent inheritance and 20 per cent environment' – are likewise meaningless unless the environment in question is carefully specified, and inferences based upon it are meticulously circumscribed. But even when specified and circumscribed, such arguments are usually both socially trivial and theoretically misconceived. They can tell us nothing about individuals, and nothing about the changes we may expect in them if the society in which they grow up is in some significant respect altered.[15]

It is easy to lose sight of the point that the environments within which human beings grow up consist of people, and of what those people believe. And while psychologists may have had little direct experimental influence over what people do, there can be not the slightest doubt that we have contributed in a massive way to what they believe. Easily the most influential aspect of this contribution has been our promotion of an attitude to upbringing, education and the running of society that is broadly liberated or free. This set of beliefs I shall call the permissive attitude; and as the chief contribution that we have so far made to our society, I shall devote the rest of this chapter to it.[16]

Since Freud laid siege to Victorian conceptions of morality,

15. Bodmer (1972) gives a clear account of the genetic background to the debate about racial differences in intelligence. Gottesman's (1968) paper is interesting, too.
16. Arguably, we have done no more than drift on a historical tide – one that has now begun to turn. My impression, though, is that our contribution has been altogether more actively polemical than this.

psychology has been identified with an attempt to banish the notions of guilt and shame, and to render the discussion of such matters humane. Whole generations of parents and teachers have been encouraged by psychologists to stop blaming, sermonizing and castigating children; and instead, to be understanding and open. At no point, we have been led to believe, should we act as the voice of society's moral law. To hold the individual morally responsible for his actions is to disregard the sufficient causes – housing, parental neglect, emotional insecurity – that have produced the behaviour of which we disapprove.

The repression and hypocrisy of Victorian society are evils that no sane person would wish to resurrect. Nevertheless, psychologists are now increasingly beginning to wonder whether the permissive attitude really is co-extensive with all that is wise and desirable. As Rollo May remarks, Freud's brand of determinism is one that reflected, rationalized, and played into the hands of, our tendency to see ourselves passively, as victims or cogs.[17] The image of man that emerged from Freud's work was of man 'not *driving* any more but *driven*'. To point, insistently, and with scientific authority, to the causes of an individual's behaviour may in practice make it increasingly difficult for him to see himself as an agent.

The permissive attitude amounts to an assault on the nineteenth century's obsession with guilt, and on the secrecy and moralizing that surrounded it. And as such, it has been sustained by a vision of Natural Man as a creature unpolluted by prudery and repression, and consequently free in two crucial respects: to work productively and to express genuine affection. But the argument is not that simple. There is a tight-rope to be walked; a balancing act to be performed. The shape of the argument is perhaps best grasped by concentrating for the moment on what happens at school. And because this is an issue that almost all of us find difficulty in discussing with even the appearance of dispassion, it is as well to begin, not with our own assumptions, but with some we find unambiguously strange.[18]

17. May (1969).
18. It is a serious question whether any body of people, academic or otherwise, can examine their own sustaining assumptions. This is perhaps especially so among psychologists and sociologists who – as Roe (1953) pointed out – are burdened with the feeling not merely of being apart from ordinary people, but of being in some vital respect superior to them.

A sharp reminder of the gulf that different systems of assumption can create comes from Urie Bronfenbrenner's comparative study of Russian and American education.[19] He looks particularly at the Russian primary school, and contrasts this pointedly with what American parents and primary-school teachers provide. Where American parents and teachers emphasize openness to experience and creativity, their Russian counterparts stress the puritan virtue of responsibility. Where American upbringing is sustained by the concept of the free individual, the Russian is sustained by that of a responsible collectivity.

Russian children are encouraged to take corporate responsibility for each other's moral welfare. This collective responsibility – alien to Western eyes – is vested, at the formal level, in Communist youth organizations, of which each classroom is a unit. There are three such organizations: the Octobrists (for ages 7 to 9), the Pioneers (10 to 15), and the Komsomol, or Young Communist League (16 to early adulthood). Membership of the Octobrists and Pioneers – unlike the Komsomol, which is more selective – is virtually universal. Hence their rules are not the prescriptions of a small club or elite; they are the regulations that govern the daily lives of the vast majority of Soviet children everywhere.

Even for seven-year-olds, the Octobrists have a formal code that leaves no doubt about the nature of Soviet society's moral requirements:

Rules of the Octobrists
1. Octobrists are future Pioneers.
2. Octobrists are diligent, study well, like school, and respect grown-ups.
3. Only those who like work are called Octobrists.
4. Octobrists are honest and truthful children.
5. Octobrists are good friends, read, draw, live happily.

The laws of the Pioneers are equally eloquent, the relevant posters especially. To the Western eye, these are naïve. They emphasize, again, discipline and courtesy, loyalty and responsibility; but there are other messages too. One picture shows a

19. Bronfenbrenner (1970).

girl handling a metal-working wrench, while a boy looks on. Work, in other words, is co-operative; it is practical; and it is shared by men and women alike. The Pioneer, another law tells us, 'loves nature': he 'is a protector of green plants, useful birds and animals'.

One poster, however, strikes us as fearsome. It positively impales you. The motto reads 'A Pioneer tells the truth and treasures the honor of his unit'. But what the picture shows is a fresh-faced young Pioneer standing, addressing both his teacher and the whole moral world about the guilty sinner lurking beside him. He points the sinner out with the index finger of his right hand. The gesture is not tensely accusatory: it has a little of the calm of a Renaissance saint. The young Pioneer, in other words, is not denouncing his form-mate; he is lifting himself by his action on to the plane of moral universals (see Plate 4).

Fortunately, Bronfenbrenner can tell us something about the ways in which this earnest sincerity is shaped. In school, competition is the norm; competition not between individuals but between groups. This competition is later extended to competition between classes, and competition between schools. At the classroom level, this competitiveness between small groups – or 'links' – is monitored by group leaders. A snippet from a Soviet teacher's manual helps to capture the tone:

Here is a typical picture. It is the beginning of the lesson. In the first row the link leader reports, basing his comments on information submitted by the sanatarian and other responsible monitors: 'Today Valodya did the wrong problem. Masha didn't write neatly and forgot to underline the right words in her lesson; Alyosha had a dirty shirt collar.' . . . The youngsters are not offended by this procedure: they understand that the link leaders are not merely tattle-telling, but simply fulfilling their duty. It doesn't even occur to the monitors and sanatarians to conceal the shortcomings of their comrades. They feel that they are doing their job well precisely when they notice one or another defect.[20]

Idealized, no doubt; but even as a textbook example, distinctly odd. Yet the adult society this educational system supports is by no means a hell-hole of emotional inhibition and social conformity. As Bronfenbrenner says, Russians seem free to express affection to children with an openness and spon-

20. Bronfenbrenner (1970), p. 60.

taneity that, in American society, would be viewed as mildly pathological:

> . . . it is not uncommon, when sitting in a crowded public conveyance, to have a child placed on your lap by a parent or guardian. Strangers strike up acquaintance with young children as a matter of course . . . Nor is the nurturant role limited to adults. Older children of both sexes show a lively interest in the very young and are competent and comfortable in dealing with them to a degree almost shocking to a Western observer. I recall an incident which occurred on a Moscow street. Our youngest son – then four – was walking briskly a pace or two ahead of us when from the opposite direction there came a company of teenage boys. The first one . . . opened his arms wide and . . . scooped him up, hugged him, kissed him resoundingly, and passed him on to the rest of the company, who did likewise . . . Similar behaviour on the part of any American adolescent male would surely prompt his parents to consult a psychiatrist.[21]

Bronfenbrenner believes, in contrast, that American parents have used the ethos of individual liberty to create a state of permissiveness for their children that amounts to neglect. American children command little of their parents' attention; and the predominant influences upon them are the television and their peers, both signally devoid of an ethical structure. Bronfenbrenner also reports that German parents are more likely than Americans to discipline their children, and to conceive of their relationship as one not of 'pals' but of parent to children. But they are also more likely to be affectionate with their children, to offer them help, and to take part with them in joint activities. The same might equally be said of French parents, where parental responsibilities, both legally and more informally, remain exacting.

The implication is that permissiveness may act against what its proponents most want for children: the freedom to work with dedication, and both to experience and express authentic affection. To this extent it may constitute a reluctance to walk the tight-rope – a denial that enables the denier to slip away from the point of tension between expression and constraint.

In attempting to state where the tight-rope is, the idea of a boundary is once more the vital one. The drift of much recent anthropological and sociological argument – for instance, Mary Douglas's – is that a sense of the conventional boundaries and

21. ibid., p. 8.

demarcations of their society is transmitted to the young by means of social ritual.[22] The function of the boundaries, in their turn, is to 'mediate' the conflicts of value on which the society is built. Extending this idea into psychology, the function of conventional boundaries becomes that of providing a matrix or format within which conflicting emotions can legitimately be expressed one at a time, in a state of mutual insulation. Where, on this argument, the conventionally bounded person expresses both desire and guilt, fluently but separately, his unbounded neighbour remains tongue-tied, because these conflicting sentiments continually mingle with one another in his mind. Likewise with the need for purity and the gratification of dirt; the longing for security and the attraction of danger; and so on. The bounded person finds ways of indulging each in turn, legitimately; the unbounded never unburdens himself satisfactorily of either.

Such a formulation may sound reactionary. And certainly, in the traditional approach to education and upbringing, lines of demarcation are strong, and discipline is seen as inherent both to bodies of knowledge (the classics, mathematics, physical science), and to the social and moral organization the teacher represents. Discipline, in other words, is something that adults impose on children: 'Break your child's will,' puritans like John Wesley recommended, 'in order that his soul may live.'[23]

The permissive attitude represents a complete contrast. The sense of structure is relatively weak, and in any case emergent rather than given. It is seen as embedded in the individual's growing sense of his own capacities and needs. And disciplinary constraints and boundaries are assumed to be mischievous until proved otherwise. Where the traditional approach is seen as a process of initiation into a system of knowledge and values that exists immutably, the more permissive one is child-centred and open to change. Where the first is based on the familiar metaphor of the walled city, the second springs from that of an encampment which evolves only as much internal organization as it demonstrably needs.

Between these two opposed philosophies, along the tight-

22. Douglas (1970); also Bernstein (1971).
23. Greven (1973) gives primary sources for the attitude of the evangelical puritans to child-raising.

rope, there lurks a third. For lack of a better word, I shall call it 'progressive'. This seeks to reconcile a strong sense of structure with a justification for it that is rational. In terms of discipline, it envisages the process of growth as one of continual adjustment and reconciliation between the two kinds of order: the one that is intrinsic to bodies of knowledge and to the structure of social life, and the one that gradually evolves in the mind of the child.

My own feeling is that this progressive position is more nearly correct than either of the other two. There are at least two reasons why the sailing may not be plain. In the first place, a parent or teacher needs formidable ingenuity and stamina if he is to produce a framework that is, at one and the same time, bindingly strong and evidently reasonable. In practice, we continually slip away from the tricky point of balance, falling back towards the traditional or permissive extremes. (Once again, the metaphor of rainwater on a pitched roof comes to mind.) More pressing are the respects in which external discipline and the criterion of perceived reasonableness conflict. There is a passage in Bertrand Russell's biography that captures one of these perfectly:

At the age of eleven, I began Euclid, with my brother as my tutor. This was one of the great events of my life, as dazzling as first love. I had not imagined that there was anything so delicious in the world . . . From that moment until Whitehead and I finished *Principia Mathematica*, when I was thirty-eight, mathematics was my chief interest, and my chief source of happiness.

But, even then, he was sensitive to the problem of reasonableness, for he goes on:

Like all happiness, however, it was not unalloyed. I had been told that Euclid proved things, and was much disappointed that he started with axioms. At first I refused to accept them unless my brother could offer me some reason for doing so, but he said: 'If you don't accept them we cannot go on', and as I wished to go on, I reluctantly admitted them *pro tem*. The doubt as to the premisses of mathematics which I felt at that moment remained with me, and determined the course of my subsequent work.[24]

If the point of view advanced in this chapter is substantially correct, the same ambiguities play around the exercises of parental authority too. 'If you don't accept it, you cannot go on.'

24. Russell (1967), p. 36.

The very reluctance of the permissive parent to exercise an arbitrary authority – to say 'This is right and that is wrong' – may cut the child off from vital advantages that the acceptance of a given framework can provide. Yet doubts can and should linger in the child's mind, as they did in Russell's; and the extent to which they are perceived and eventually acted upon helps to shape what kinds of people we become.

The key features of the genuinely progressive position are the consistent exercise of authority by the parent or teacher, and the elaboration of a system of negotiable boundaries and reticences appropriate to a hierarchy of generations. These create a stable framework, and they can be justified in three ways. In terms of their surface properties; the sense, for instance, of reasonableness or elegance that we perceive in them. Or in terms of their hidden implications; the extent to which, say, they originate in the broader experience of the parent as a parent, the teacher as a teacher. Or, quite practically, in terms of their 'pay-off'; whether, as a matter of fact, they do or do not promote the expression of affection, or the ability to cope with guilt.[25]

Before abandoning the permissive attitude and its authoritarian antithesis, there are two of its concomitants that I would like briefly to mention, because I have not seen these discussed adequately elsewhere.

The first of these is the connection between permissiveness in the intellectual sphere and the democratic desire to break down snobbish social distinctions. One of the earliest comments on this link was made by the American critic Lionel Trilling in response, as it happens, to Kinsey's work on sex. Kinsey's urge to liberate us from sexual prudery ends, Trilling claims, in the tacit endorsement of a 'democratic pluralism of sexuality': a desire to habituate the reader to sexuality in its every shape and form. But such pluralism is less liberating than it seems, because it goes with 'a nearly conscious aversion from making intellectual distinctions, almost as if out of the belief that an intellectual distinction must inevitably lead to a social discrimination

25. And, in each respect, we may reach ambiguities: a permissive regime (like that at Summerhill) may work wonders for maladjusted children, but poorly with more ordinary ones: Neill (1968). A traditional regime may encourage intellectual excitement (as in Russell), but at the expense of more personal gratification.

or exclusion'.[26] It is just this assumption that intellectual distinctions imply snobbish social ones, that is one of the most puzzling features of the academic life of our time. Yet why it should have sprung up, and why it should influence so many people who are otherwise sharp-witted, is not altogether clear to me.

The second adjunct to permissiveness that interests me concerns that ogre of the liberated: the censor. Thinking back to the vicious circle mentioned in Chapter 5 it seems clear that young people in a state of anomie are ripe both for commercial and also for political exploitation. And the direction of this exploitation can be positively pathological. The instance that sticks in my mind is, in practical terms, a slender one; but important because it catches psychologists so consistently on the wrong foot – reacting ideologically, rather than thinking with care.

The *Little Red School-Book* is a text written in simple language by two Danes, addressing themselves to school-children, and enlightening them about how to survive in a world run by adults.[27] They are concerned to 'demystify' the relations of children with their parents and teachers; and – a dominant preoccupation – to banish guilt about sex. Most Western countries have attempted to censor the book; and for this reason if for no other, its authors seem to enjoy the intuitive support of almost every young and enlightened psychologist and social scientist I know.

Whether the book can or ought to be censored, I do not know – and do not much care. But it does seem to me that it is, of itself, unpleasant; and that it is at least arguable that the world would be a better place without it. Throughout, its tone, though hinting at the tongue in cheek, is relentlessly explicit, and relentlessly reductive.[28] Especially disquieting is the hostility that it predicates between children and adults. The authors assume – for instance, in their comments about masturbation – that adults are liars rather than merely misinformed or embarrassed. If an adult tells them not to 'do it too much', children are advised to

26. Trilling (1954). As a commentary on Kinsey's reaction to the extreme puritanism of his own upbringing, this strikes me as quite exceptionally shrewd – see, for example, Pomeroy (1967).
27. Hansen and Jensen (1971).
28. A veneer of jokiness is a useful component of any persuasive package. As in the telling of anti-Semitic jokes, critics can always be turned away with 'Oh, don't take it so *seriously*'.

retort by asking 'how often you ought to do it', because 'they'll usually shut up then'. This proposition makes what I take to be an obscene assumption: namely that when the occasion demands, children should be ready to knock adults from their pedestals with a deft and unanswerable verbal thrust.

It would be an error to make too much of this scruffy little offering. As Winnicott says, 'there is something better than knowledge about sex, and that is the discovery of it by the individual'.[29] The *Little Red School-Book* none the less sheds an unhappy light on the system of self-evident virtues it claims to represent. In its eagerness to expunge guilt, to deny it any legitimate existence, the permissive attitude shows alarming tendencies to trust only what is down-to-earth and physical; and also to evade the dilemmas of parental authority, sliding away into suggestions about 'democracy', and, when these fail, into the rhetoric of political confrontation. Yet it is presumably on parental love and trust, rather than on the brazen arts of negotiation, or on a flow of accurate information about reproductive biology, that the welfare of children depends.

The danger, conceptually speaking, lies in establishing the idea of freedom as a simple and overriding criterion for deciding the day-to-day tactics of upbringing, rather than using it as a component part of a more distant goal. Pursued literally, it leads to the denial of necessary tension and paradox, with results that can be both intellectually stultifying, and even downright nasty. Analogous consequences would seem to flow when we slip off the roof into the opposing gutter, and single-mindedly pursue the idea, not of freedom but of authority. As evidence, one need only think of the barbarities of the old-fashioned English boarding-school – the ritualized bullying and humiliation, and the corporal punishment by one boy of another. Or the inhumanity, in the past at least, of life in a military academy. Or, altogether more extreme, the more all-embracing obscenities of the Hitler youth movement. But such excesses require no rehearsal: we already have them fully in focus. It is on our own areas of smugness and conceptual laziness that we would be wise to dwell.

29. Winnicott (1964), p. 216. Winnicott also protests, surely correctly, that 'it is no use telling children in groups that to masturbate is not harmful, because perhaps for one of the group it *is* harmful, compulsive, and a great nuisance, in fact evidence of psychiatric illness'.

Among these, I very strongly suspect, is the assumption that, as parents or teachers, the use of moral rather than factual categories should be taboo. To treat a child in terms of the external causes that play upon him, is half-way to envisaging him as a cog; and to treat him as a cog is more than half-way towards ceasing to care in any profound or personal way about him. It is as agents, not cogs, that we react vividly to each other. Accordingly, whilst recognizing the causal influences that play on the child, and taking them into account, the adult ought to feel free to talk to children in moral terms – indeed, it may be for this very purpose that moral language was in the first place evolved. And this, not for the sake of a sober and stable society, not to render the adult's life convenient, but to ensure, as best we can, that the child will grow up to enjoy his own agent-hood – and, through that agent-hood, to enjoy a sense of gratification in the ordinary texture of his life that is real and immediate rather than ersatz.

12 Our Intimate Relations

It is one thing to criticize permissive and more authoritarian attitudes as simplistic and therefore potentially dangerous. It is another to suggest how, in practice and in detail, the ambivalences of desire and guilt might be managed better. In Chapter 14 I shall attempt something of the sort, concentrating there on the world of the arts, and, more generally, on the constructive use that we can sometimes make of our brains. My purpose here, though, is more cautious, and conceivably a little cowardly. The focus is on that intimate and exclusive form of relationship that takes its paradigmatic shape in the Western marriage.[1] And, in particular, on certain sorts of crises that such relationships often undergo. But rather than offering any general view of why such personal crises arise, I want to say something about the form they take, and to establish certain of the interpretative concepts that they force us to use.

In doing this, I may seem to step rather abruptly from the relatively public and commonsensical world of upbringing and education into waters that are altogether murkier and more mysterious. This apparent shift in the level of the discussion is a consequence, I think, of the efforts we make as a culture to disguise from ourselves what personal intimacy consists of. It is of course true that many intimacies are in part physically sexual. Also that, more personally, they raise practical-sounding issues of 'adjustment' and 'compatibility'. But to leave the discussion of our personal lives at this physical or quasi-physical level, is to gloss over all those aspects of them that are most important to us. For such relationships characteristically depend on an emotionally charged traffic of glance and gesture; and it is on this traffic that the blossoming or withering of each relationship depends.

1. Like much else, an institution that is beginning to change: Rapoport and Rapoport (1969).

This is not to say that personal intimacy is a matter of delicate shades and fine sentiments. Far from it. But these aspects of our lives do seem to turn on detail and nuance; points of focus that carry a burden of emotional significance out of all proportion to their literal meaning. It follows that those aspects of our personal lives that are most real to us are precisely those that are the most difficult to pin down for the purposes of literal-minded research. (And for this reason, the territory as a whole is one that behaviourists and positivists have both been at pains to avoid.) In establishing the lie of such land, even in terms of literary or philosophical example, we are forced to cut ourselves loose from the public criteria of truth and falsity that govern our statements about what people can be seen to do. In some, this induces agoraphobic dismay. Yet we know in practice that this freedom from public criteria does not leave us entirely disorientated. We have other markers and reference points; and it is these that I shall be touching on in the next few pages – using ideas like 'emotional honesty', 'authenticity', and 'self-deception', which refer to aspects of our everyday competence, but which, within the strictly behavioural view of psychology, are meaningless.

Although techniques exist for exploring the processes of our private lives, these are exceptionally clumsy to use.[2] In the short run there is more to be learnt from a novelist like Doris Lessing, who views personal intimacy with an unusually analytic eye. Her portrait of the collapsing union between Martha and Douglas in *A Proper Marriage* places our feet firmly on the appropriate ground:

Loyalty towards love was forcing her to pretend that she was not disappointed, and that she did not – at that moment she was sick with repulsion – find him repulsive. But already that image of a lover that a woman is offered by society, and carries with her so long, had divorced itself from Douglas, like the painted picture of a stencil floating off paper in water. Because that image remained intact and unhurt, it was possible to be good-natured. It is that image which keeps so many marriages peaceable and friendly.[3]

The metaphor of a stencil floating off paper in water and remaining fragile but intact, is wonderfully apposite. It is this stencil that permits otherwise grossly dissonant personal

2. For example, the Interpersonal Perception Method: Laing *et al.* (1966).
3. Lessing (1966), p. 35.

relationships to survive in a condition of mutual friendliness and toleration. Though socially useful, stencils none the less permit discrepancies of perception to grow – and with them a sense of estrangement: an alienation that hollows out a relationship while, to all intents and purposes, it continues on its successful way. The loyalty to love is compounded in its effect, Lessing later suggests, by the necessity many women experience, however bored or disillusioned they are, to be 'good in bed'. She speaks of the hundreds of thousands of women in our society who, however jaded they become, still pin their faith in a 'determined hedonism' – an 'accomplished athleticism' that quiets all suspicions by the 'variety and ingenuity of the physical attitude it recommends':

Douglas could hardly be blamed for not understanding the thoroughness of Martha's dislike for him, since that prohibition prevented her from ever expressing it in bed. The moment she did so, it would have meant the complete collapse of the romantic picture she maintained of him. A young woman of this type will expend immense energy on arranging her image of her husband into something admirable and attractive. And this is a question of principle. Such a young woman will confuse all bystanders by being charmingly devoted to her husband . . . until the very moment she leaves him. After which she will not have one good word to say for him.[4]

As Philip Larkin's poem 'Talking in Bed' puts it: 'Talking in bed ought to be easiest, lying together there goes back so far'; but 'it becomes still more difficult to find words at once true and kind, or not untrue and not unkind'.

In her story *A Charmed Life*, Mary McCarthy portrays another Martha – also at a crisis point.[5] And she does so in a way which enables us to see how, in such situations, practical implications are interwoven with moral ones. Martha Sinnott, now married to John Sinnott, allows herself one evening to be violently seduced by her ex-husband Miles Murphy. The encounter leaves her wrought up but unfulfilled (and also, incidentally, pregnant). When her husband returns, Martha acknowledges to herself the implications that sexual intercourse with him would bear. It would be perfectly possible, but, she believes, in an important sense wrong, to go through with him their by

4. Lessing (1966), p. 309.
5. McCarthy (1956).

156

now somewhat humdrum intimacies, while still inflamed in imagination by her encounter with Miles: an encounter that John did not know about, and which, had he known, would have disturbed him deeply.

The situation is real, in the sense that we recognize the predicament Mary McCarthy describes. Such options may not have presented themselves to us personally; but, tacitly, we acknowledge that, if they had, they would have faced us with decisions that are only in part practical.

There is, of course, no behaviouristic account of the thoughts passing through Martha's mind. If consistent, a behaviourist must ignore them. Yet dilemmas like Martha's contain a whole algebra of circumstance and implication, valuable for the interpretative categories they impose upon us. And it is from just this area that the materialist wants to edge us away: talk of revelation, deception and self-deception, and of the moral and aesthetic standards whereby almost all our more important personal decisions are made. This is the area in which a philosophy like Gilbert Ryle's, designed to curtail the discussion of mental events, becomes so awkward as to verge on the silly;[6] while the existential and phenomenological traditions of Continental Europe come more nearly into their own.[7]

As our concern is conceptual, let us leave the two Marthas, Douglas, John and Miles, and adopt in their place two cyphers, Jacques and Jill; and we shall proceed in the best spirit of the philosopher's example.[8] Jacques and Jill, let us assume, are overlapping octagons: they treat their relationship as the context within which all their more profound aspirations for themselves are set. Their marriage, like any other, is a matter of acts and cravings that are ambiguously those of the imagination and of the body too. It is an area where 'is' and 'ought' become confused; the ideal stamping-ground, you would have thought, for philosopher and psychologist alike. Yet the materialistic conception of human relations has such a grip on us that we find it hard to form plain sentences that describe this everyday

6. Ryle (1949).
7. Particularly perhaps the work of Merleau-Ponty (1962). Though somewhat solipsistic in tone, he avoids Sartre's clever pessimism, and also the sense that Sartre conveys of playing gratuitously with words.
8. A different but complementary use of such cyphers will be found in Laing (1961), (1970).

phenomenon: the exclusive commitment that most of us make to another person.

Assume, by no means frivolously, that Jacques' intimacies with Jill are moving into a crisis state. While Jacques is in bed with Jill, he experiences yearnings about someone other than Jill: Jill's friend Olive. And while Jacques has fantasies about Olive, Jill pictures herself in the arms of Jacques' friend Fred. Their bed, in other words, contains four people, not two. Three intimate acts occur; not one. And of these three acts, only one forms part of the knowledge that we can assume Jacques and Jill share.[9] The *dramatis personae* can multiply itself still further, of course; and the pattern of plot and sub-plot can become diversified. Jacques may entertain fantasies about a whole gallery of people besides Olive; and in those fantasies, he may fill a variety of roles. Jill likewise. And it is for this reason that matrimony has been described as 'serial polygamy with one person'.

As the philosopher Karl Popper has acknowledged, we are all philosophers after our fashion.[10] We all make assumptions about what is real, and about what we see as our fault – as part of our personal responsibility. These are, respectively, our own personal ontological and ethical systems. Jacques and Jill may differ in these respects; both from each other, and ourselves. Jacques sees his fantasies as real – as an aspect of his life that is more pressingly vivid to him than any other; but he denies all guilt about them, and sees them as lying beyond his responsibility. His fantasies about Olive seem to Jacques like a visitation over which he has no control. Jill, on the other hand, sees her scenes with Fred as unreal; but, none the less, as a feature of her mental life for which she feels responsible, and about which she is deeply concerned. Jacques copes with dissonance and anxiety by dissociating himself ethically, while Jill copes by dissociating herself ontologically. Jacques denies that his fantasies are his fault; Jill denies that hers are really there.

These informal philosophies have point because they influence

9. The question of which of these three acts is the real one is patently foolish: each is, after its fashion. Nor is this all. Buber has remarked of the erotic life that 'in no other realm are dialogue and monologue so mingled and opposed'. Around the dialogue that Jacques and Jill share, or at least partially share, there play their own respective monologues – fantasies that overlay and often conflict with the versions of the dialogue that each entertains.

10. Popper (1972).

the moves that each individual will make. Two issues are especially important: whether illicit fantasies or desires are acknowledged, and whether they are acted upon. Each opens up a further set of options. Jacques may or may not tell Jill about Olive. Likewise, Jill about Fred. If disclosed, the fantasies themselves may change; and the tone of the relationship may alter. A sense of magic may evaporate, leaving the union seeming prosaic. Or, conversely, the revelations might dispel an air of falsity; the relationship, as a consequence, may seem less precarious, more real, and the sharing of polygamous fantasies may become part of what that relationship consists of.

At present, we are more or less totally ignorant about the paths such events are likely to follow. For the sake of exposition, let us postulate that Jill can no longer deny her fantasies about Fred. Rather than disclosing them to Jacques, she acts upon them: she goes to bed with Fred. Now to cross from the world of fantasy to that of action is to cross the boundary around which the ethical requirements of our culture come most sharply into focus – it is one thing to be tempted, quite another to succumb. It is also the boundary around which our senses of expectation and grievance coalesce. As we take a clear step towards someone we desire, we enter a realm of stubborn inconvenience, in which their commitments are always tangential to our own. Events fall short of expectations; and the rosier the expectations, the greater the mutilation they suffer. What we achieve in this world of stubborn inconvenience, we achieve by negotiation and compromise; and the structure that results will be one into which our fantasies must squeeze themselves as best they can.[11]

Again for the sake of exposition, let us say that Jill enjoys her venture across this boundary. She feels she has learnt through this new relationship about herself and about life; but comes to realize that Fred-in-the-flesh does not live up to Fred-in-the-mind's-eye. For the time being, the affair with Fred ends.

Jill's position is a delicate one. Should she make a 'clean breast' of it to Jacques? A number of thoughts will weigh with her. Some are straightforward: the principle that the truth

11. It seems that the only way in which we can realize our fantasies without rupturing their integrity is by translating them into the language of the arts. More of that in Chapter 14.

should be told, the likelihood of scandal and uproar, the thought of hurting Jacques. Others are more elusive. These will include matters of judgment about her own feelings, and about the state of the two pertinent relationships – what she feels for Jacques, what she thinks he feels for her, and the prospects for their relationship in the future. Similarly apropos Fred. For even though her relation with him is over, she may still be influenced by her commitment to the aspects of her own character she discovered with him.

Harder still to pin down, yet potentially just as influential, are the existential aspects of Jill's predicament. Three possibilities are particularly worth mentioning. The first of these concerns her sense of Jacques' dignity. To protect him from the truth may well be, in her eyes, to belittle or degrade him; to set him up as a cuckold. In addition, she may well have to weigh her feelings of guilt. She may find guilt intolerable and assume that any way of dissipating it, however painful, is better than none. Conversely, the very act of doing something that seems to her wrong may have been a liberating step: a liberation that would be compromised or lost by revelation. And, thirdly, she may find herself considering her sense of her own separateness. To tell all, to spill the beans to Jacques, may simply be to avoid the final responsibility for being a separate person.

And notice the language that such possibilities force us to use. Much of it is implicitly moral; much of it rests on ideas like honesty, where these refer to states of mind of an elusive variety. The extent of this elusiveness comes home to us if we commit Jill to further deception.

She neglects to tell Jacques about her affair with Fred; and when asked point-blank about it, she denies it out of hand. As spectators and arbiters, our dilemma is that we do not know how to react. We lack the necessary information about her motives. She could be an unprincipled pragmatist: someone who lies easily, who steers round trouble, and to whom issues of principle or human dignity are largely empty. Or she may have been moved, against every inclination to tell the truth, to take upon herself the full burden of guilt and dissonance for what she has done. Jacques is deceived. But the moral and psychological fabric of the two situations is as dissimilar as any two could be: one rather squalid; the other, in a mixed and modest way, slightly heroic. To decide which applies in fact to Jill, we would have to get to know her very well indeed.

This cameo poses two sorts of question that – in our capacity as research workers – we do our best to skirt round. The question of what is psychologically honest, true or authentic; and the question of what help or advice one person can give another.

To a certain extent, psychological honesty is a matter of disclosure and representation. Jill may or may not make clear to Jacques what her feelings about Fred are. But even here, in talking to Jacques about what she did and what she felt, she will be offering both as a *construction*: a quasi-theatrical conception of her role, in which she will believe with more or less conviction.[12] If we refer back to what Eileen Atkins said about acting in Chapter 7, we see that this is not a matter of pretence; but it *is* a matter of finding a story that is convincing – both to the actress and to her audience. In other words, being honest, for Jill, is in essence a matter of being true to herself; of being true to her own nature. In deciding what to say and do, she is assembling thoughts about who she is and what she stands for: and the dissonance she is attempting to resolve is not between a fact and her representation of it, but between what her true nature is and her construction of it.[13]

But there is more delving to be done. For Jill can deceive not only Jacques, but herself as well. And such self-deception characteristically takes the shape of a collective 'conspiracy'; the creation of a world of make-believe. The unhappy characters in John Osborne's play *Look Back in Anger* try to create a haven from their mutual incompatibility in a myth-world in which she is a squirrel, he a bear. It is said that Winston Churchill, who had relatively little time for women, played a game with his wife that they were cats. Fictions like this steer couples round the reefs; and may go on doing so for a lifetime. Equally though, they can come to seem false; and this falsity can come to seem intolerable.

It was probably just such falseness that Jill stepped outside,

12. The 'constructed' nature of such vital exchanges is stressed by Berger and Kellner (1971).
13. The relation of authenticity to self-disclosure is explored by Laing (1961); also Jourard (1964).

when she plunged into her affair with Fred. Her life with Jacques seemed boring; but boring because it was in vital respects artificial. Accordingly, Fred and Jill banished 'phoniness'. They related to one another on the basis of carnal passion. But this, Jill realized, was itself a construction, a myth-world no less convention-bound than the one from which she had just escaped. It 'wasn't her'. Quite rapidly, the whole business of being un-inhibitedly physical took on the air of a charade. With Fred, she got something out of her system: the release of a person pent up by years of playing anxiously at squirrels and bears, which evaporated quite quickly once she was no longer wholly dependent on Jacques. In retrospect, the self she was with Fred, came to seem 'split' from who she really was. A figment.[14] And whether she realizes it or not, her fantasies about Fred – even her affair with him – may well have been akin to her squirrel and bear games, in that all three were devices that enabled her to continue her relationship with Jacques without coming to grips with its inherent structure of reciprocal dependencies and needs.

Intuitively, again, we know that discriminations of this sort are real; and we demonstrate that intuitive acknowledgment by our readiness to judge Jill for the ways in which she reacts. Our sensitivities, in fact, are alerted on at least four fronts:

1. We are poised to react sceptically if she places a 'high' construction of what we suspect to be a 'low' motive: sceptical, for instance, if she holds forth about her integrity, or identity, when we suspect that she is in fact moved by snobbery, greed, or lust.

2. Equally, we are dubious if a 'low' construction is put on a motive that we believe is in some sense 'higher'. A whole rhetoric of reductively sexual interpretations exist for men to swap with one another – explaining as a matter of lust what are often, as far as one can tell, yearnings of more complex variety: a fear of old age, for example, or of death.

3. An account may often strike us, too, as excessively theatrical. A certain style or sweep we accept, but we grow distrustful if Jill offers herself in one of the more melodramatic roles: 'heroine', say, or 'martyr'.

14. The concepts of 'true' and 'false self' have semi-technical meanings in phenomenological psychology; Laing (1960), (1961) offers the clearest exposition that I know of.

4. Likewise if Jill talks about herself in terms that are too self-conscious or explicit. If she produces a line of prattle about her 'father fixation' or her 'identity crisis', we would suspect self-indulgence – and resent the devaluation of an already precarious currency.

We touch here on cultural differences, and on matters of taste. Those granted, we none the less know that in watching Jill and listening to her we are ready to appraise her.[15] We also know, sometimes to our own puzzlement and chagrin, that we will respond favourably to her if we see her as living full-bloodedly, according to her own lights – even though those lights are ones of which we disapprove.

In a moment of desperation, Jill might turn to a friend for advice, or to a professional psychotherapist. We must now come to grips with the categories we use in deciding whether that help and advice is good or bad. If she goes to a professional, she will almost certainly be encouraged to see her fantasies and fears as normal and natural. She will be encouraged to worry about them no more than she can help; and to do her best to make what she is worried about explicit. As a purely cerebral exercise, this will probably do more good than harm. 'Words and gestures,' after all, 'are the most delicate instruments we have and are likely to remain so for a long while.'[16]

None the less, the benefits will in all probability remain limited unless the therapeutic relationship becomes one of mutual trust: unless, that is, the therapist becomes in Jill's eyes – and perhaps his own – a genuine rival to Jacques and Fred for her affections. Freud's ideal of therapy has been described as a form of psychic surgery – the removal from the mind of morbidly disruptive fantasies, leaving the individual free to return to healthy rationality. But as Jung realized, 'we cannot simply extract . . . morbidity like a foreign body . . . Our task is not to weed it out, but to cultivate and transform this growing thing until it can play its part in the totality of the psyche.' The therapist is no longer 'the agent of treatment but a fellow

15. There is no more scrupulous analyst of such falsities than the novelist Angus Wilson.
16. Joyce (1972).

participant in a process of individual development'. The patient discovers 'who he really is' by reconciling the opposed forces at work within him – forces that, while unresolved, prevent him from coping with those situations that his present life forces upon him:

If I wish to treat another individual psychologically at all, I must for better or worse give up all pretensions to superior knowledge, all authority and desire to influence. I must perforce adopt a dialectical procedure consisting in a comparison of our mutual findings.[17]

A recognition of this reciprocally personal basis of psycho-therapy is growing among therapists themselves: in the accept-ance by Peter Lomas, for instance, that the intimate relation of therapist to patient is at root no different from many other intimacies. On this view, all substantial personal changes are mediated by intimate personal relationships; and the ideal therapeutic relation is one in which the patient is able to use the mutual affection and trust that he and the therapist feel for one another in developing a sense of responsibility for his own actions.[18] And attempts that the orthodox Freudian psycho-analysts have made to escape from this intimacy – to call it the 'transference', and treat it as a one-sided and essentially illusory part of the patient's neurosis, are a fraud. This is especially but not exclusively so, where patient and therapist are of opposite sexes. Szasz has made this point with clarity in his dissection of the problems of containment that the pioneers like Freud and Breuer faced:

Thus, as Breuer proceeded in translating Anna O.'s symptoms into the language of personal problems, he found it necessary to carry on a relationship with her without the protection previously afforded by the hysterical symptoms ... So long as the patient was unaware of dis-turbing affects and needs – especially aggressive and erotic – she could not openly disturb her physician with them. But once these inhibitions were lifted – or, as we might say, once the translation was effected – it

17. Roazen (1975), p. 273. As in other respects, Jung seems here much closer to current practice than does Freud himself. It is hard to avoid the impression that, after Jung's split with Freud in 1913, the orthodox launched a success-ful campaign to discredit both him and his views – an exercise in the political arts, it must be confessed, in which Freud himself played a significant part. Ernest Jones, Freud's biographer, seems to have been especially shameless, his apparent good sense and impartiality masking a zealous determination to forward the Freudian cause. Roazen's appears a more balanced view.
18. The best introductions that I know to the current state of psychoanalysis are both British: Rycroft (1968) and Lomas (1973).

became necessary for the therapist to deal with the new situation: a sexually aroused attractive *woman*, rather than a pitifully disabled *patient*.

Breuer, it appears, was overcome by the 'reality' of his relationship with Anna O. The threat of the patient's eroticism was effectively tamed by Freud when he created the concept of transference: the analyst could henceforth tell himself that he was not the genuine object, but a mere symbol, of his patient's desire.[19]

The 'transference' is real and it is important: in therapy as in ordinary life, each person will perceive the other to some extent (or even wholly) as a figment of fantasy. But such a relationship *is* reciprocal; and usually there is more afoot. However throttled or distorted, there exists the need to break out of the cocoon that such fantasies create around us – to enter, in this case, into a relationship in which sexual passion can be physically expressed.

Depending on how well she and her therapist manage such unruly needs, Jill may find herself enjoying a sense of trust which enables her to plot out the cardinal relations in her life; and, in particular, the shape of her relationship with Jacques – not just the present irritation and boredom, but its underlying structure. This will involve both her and her therapist in complicated processes of reconstruction – ones in which, as the philosophers of science are fully aware, the distinction between a good and a bad reconstruction is often hard to draw.

The boredom and irritation that now force themselves on Jill will almost certainly have arisen from what she sees as temperamental incompatibilities between herself and Jacques. Jacques, let us say, is a man whose social presence is that of someone highly impulsive; but in whom, below this surface, there lurk deep reserves of prudence and self-control. Jill exemplifies the reverse pattern. Her social presence is cautious; but in matters of more profound significance, she is prone to plunge, to commit herself to a person or a cause without reservation. Jacques and Jill consequently construe their love for one another as based on the attraction of opposites; but, in retrospect, she sees the bond as more complex. She now believes that she saw her own buried impulsiveness reflected in Jacques' surface impulsivity; while he saw his own buried caution reflected in her social reserve. And

19. Szasz (1962b), pp. 438 and 443.

both envisaged a delightful melting together, in which their own internal contradictions would be resolved.[20]

And what went wrong between them sprang from just these same contradictions. Two systems of mutual doubt gradually took shape. Jill found herself scared that Jacques would see her as boring and dowdy; while Jacques began to worry that Jill would see him as racketty and cheap. And, at the level of hidden motives and needs, Jill began to worry that Jacques did not really care for her deeply after all; while Jacques feared that Jill's commitment could end by engulfing him. And as 'paranoid systems' tend to, these mutual doubts gathered strength with time. What is more, the lives of the two partners began to conform to their own fears. Jacques' behaviour did in fact become somewhat cheap, and Jill really did become scruffy. Jacques' affection cooled; and Jill became committed in an even more demanding way.

Naturally, it is one matter for Jill to assemble this story about herself; quite another to use it as the basis for therapeutic action. For it may be that their mutual suspicion and fear have done irreparable harm; or it may be that their relationship was bound to fail, and is one that no one should attempt to repair. And the point is important, because, beyond kindness and insight, her therapist may go on to suggest to Jill that she should aim at a more 'mature' relationship with Jacques. That her conflicts and perplexities should, if possible, be worked through in the context of her relationship with him.

The word 'mature' should set us on guard; like 'natural' and 'normal', it seems to refer to an established body of knowledge about what is healthily human, but in fact expresses a set of values. What is more, the programme of 'working through' seems at times to be at variance with the body of understanding from which its authority is tacitly drawn: namely psychoanalysis. And this is something we should be clear about: we should know what the practical implications of the psychoanalytic vision are.

If, in the context of traditional therapy, psychoanalysis has

20. Such contradictions would seem to be a widespread – even a universal – aspect of our psychical organization. Yet you can read great tracts of the literature on personality theory without seeing them mentioned, let alone discussed. A notable exception is the work of Jung: Storr (1973). For some of the more routine work in this field, see Winch (1963).

truths of enduring value to convey to us, these take the form of two rather general propositions. The first of these, put forward with the circumstantial support of biology, holds that many of our seemingly insubstantial needs are deep-rooted and influential to a degree. The paradigmatic instance is our sense of our own gender. The second proposition, this time advanced with the massive and by no means entirely circumstantial evidence of anthropology, is that, within the nuclear family, there exists an organization that centres on the incest taboo.

Granted that we must work out with strangers – that is, those outside the family – the needs that have taken shape within it, it can scarcely surprise us if the relationships we do create contain elements of strain. The desires and prohibitions inherent in the relation of the infant to his parents generate conflicts of affection and distaste: love and hate. Consequently, we may envisage two Oedipal wishes: the incestuous and the murderous. As usual, Norman Brown has a compelling metaphor: 'coitus', he says, 'is always a funeral feast . . . on or beside a grave'.

Yet to confront the contradictions internal to any intimate relation is to confront their points of origin; and this is easy ground to stray upon only for the psychopathically inured. If we acknowledge the two messages of psychoanalysis, the whole process of mutual attraction between strangers – of falling in love, and of creating a new nuclear arrangement for the next generation – is fraught with danger. Jacques could have fallen for Jill because she aroused in him subterranean echoes of his mother; or for quite the opposite reason – because she promised to insulate him decisively from any such stirrings. In the first case, he may find that he has chosen to sit too close to the primordial fire; in the second, so far away as to suffer a sense of emptiness and boredom. The same risks will have applied to Jill. What is more, their covert needs may well conflict: Jill may want to edge Jacques towards the fire, when he already suspects that he is sitting too close.

The marriage of Jacques and Jill works itself out, then, in a hall of reverberations and echoes: it is the enactment, if it succeeds, of a drama which allows both participants to reconcile their sense of the desirable with their sense of the forbidden. Its success resides, in its turn, in the extent to which it enables the two of them to distinguish their more superficial fantasies from their profounder needs. It is precisely these reverberations and echoes that the great love poet John Donne captures. The last couplet of his 'Love's Alchymie' is perhaps the most ferociously deft in the whole language:

> Hope not for minde in women; at their best
> Sweetnesse and wit, they are but *Mummy*, possest.

Hidden beneath the surface of this easy disillusion, there lurks a positive welter of complementary insinuations. The last two words, separated by a comma, carry the implication of incestuous passion. Also, jarring harshly, the vision of necrophilia – of intercourse with a body mummified. In addition, less recondite in Donne's day than ours, there is the pun on 'mummy', 'mummae' being a word betokening an aphrodisiac. There are other ambiguities besides; but these are enough. Between them they harness, too close for any man's comfort, the fantasies that sexual relationships draw upon.

Given the delicacy of these relations between the exciting and dull, forbidden and legitimate, any simple therapeutic recipe must be arbitrary. The possibility must exist that the more Jill works through her problem, the more dispassionately she looks at Jacques, and herself in relation to him, the more surely she becomes convinced that she married the wrong person; that she can only come to terms with the prospect of spending the rest of her life with him at the expense of every sentiment she holds dear. The search for maturity can thus become an exercise in the abdication of authentic desire. To quote from Jules Henry again: '. . . in Western culture maturity is merely the capacity to mislead and avoid being misled'. And it is just this manipulative competence one would hate to see substituted, in Jill's case or any other, for the full-blooded expression of authentic need.[21]

Jill's life, I would argue, is less a story of progress along the highroad of life towards maturity, or towards any of the other versions of the Happy Ending that the ethic of progress holds up to us; more one of negotiating conflicting necessities – of finding a route past Scylla and Charybdis, across the troubled waters that lie between them. This view is quite at odds with the assumption, now popular on both sides of the Atlantic, that

21. Henry (1966), p. 274.

personal tensions can be construed as obstacles in our path – as 'problems' to be resolved. In our personal lives, tensions, I would argue, are not only unavoidable, but potentially productive. To conceive of them within the quasi-technological rhetoric of 'problem-solving' is to abandon whatever purchase upon them we might initially possess. The belief, implicit in the idea of progress, that a good life lies ahead of us – a good life that is our rightful inheritance, and that we can reach by solving our problems – seems to me a specious fiction. In contrast, the gratifications implicit in the dialectical vision are altogether more immediate and more substantial – those, namely, of negotiating the troubled waters for a while, and doing so in good style.

13   Sanity and Madness

Almost as a footnote to this discussion of our personal lives, and as a bridge to my last chapter, in which I will talk about works of art and the needs they satisfy, I want to devote a few pages to the distinction between sanity and madness. The emphasis now placed on this issue in most books about psychology with a humanistic bias seems to me disproportionate. In particular, I would like to steer clear of any suggestion that the neurotic or psychotic person is the hero of our age; likewise the notion that we are all the victims of some malign process of 'labelling' – whereby our psychic lives are controlled by the ascriptions that others impose upon us. None the less, there does seem to be a kernel of excellent good sense buried in some of the recent writing about madness, and it is one that I would like to rescue from beneath its attendant propaganda.[1]

To do this, I shall concentrate on a single work: Laing and Esterson's *Sanity, Madness and the Family*.[2] This is a most imaginative piece of research, and it presents the strongest case I know of in favour of the transactional (or 'double-bind') theory of insanity. What the authors did, quite simply, was to interview members of a small number of families, in each of which there was one person who, by conventional criteria, was mad. Finding evidence of distorted and contradictory patterns of communication in these families, the authors used this as the foundation of a phenomenological account of how people are driven out of their senses. On the basis of their work, and other material like

1. Humanistic psychology has recently become identified with efforts designed to break down the individual's sense of his own autonomy – by means, for instance, of the encounter group. This enterprise seems to me misguided; and carried to the extreme – as, for example, in the 'crotch-eyeballing' described with commendable distaste by Braginsky and Braginsky (1974) – it is grotesque.
2. Laing and Esterson (1964).

it, a number of claims about the nature of madness are now made. I want here to focus on three of these – the three that seem to me to be of the most psychological significance. These are:

1. That far from being arbitrary or salad-like, the mad person's thought processes make good sense, both in that they are coherent, and in that they represent a rational response to the wholly illogical pressures being exerted on him by others. Madness, in other words, is an 'intellible' response to an untenable situation.

2. That the victims of such pressure do not just go mad, they are driven mad – and driven there, characteristically, by their parents.

3. That people have a right to go mad, for the ordeal may well be one that leads them to greater authenticity of experience.

These claims have exerted a massive influence in psychiatry and psychology; and they now form part of a quite new conception of mental illness and its treatment. Many objections can of course be raised against them: that they glamorize madness, and gloss over both its suffering and its profound strangeness; that they heap blame on parents; that they rest on a high-handed selection of cases and of evidence about them; and so on. Rather than compiling a list of all the possible lines of protest against studies like Laing and Esterson's, I would like to concentrate on just one. The objection, namely, that they can justifiably conclude nothing about what goes on inside 'mad' families unless they first contrast these with 'sane' families – families, that is to say, in which someone has not become deranged.

Among psychologists, this objection acts like a litmus paper, separating the traditional from the newly enlightened. For defenders of Laing and the phenomenological method see the demand for comparisons with a 'control group' as an irrelevance; as evidence, in fact, that the objector has failed to grasp what Laing and Esterson have achieved. For Laing and Esterson would want to say that they have cut themselves free from the old-fashioned preoccupation with causes and with the clutter of pseudo-scientific experiment. Instead, they offer illumination: they show us what is really going on. And in turning their backs on the traditional preoccupation with causes, they are quite even-handed, ignoring genetic and psychoanalytic sorts of explanation equally.

I have to confess that my own position in this debate is a somewhat traditional one. But it is so not because I favour old 'organic' views of mental illness at the expense of the Laingian view. Rather, because I feel that through their reluctance to make comparisons, they are led to make claims of subtly the wrong kind. More generally, I would want to argue that it is the carefully poised comparison that lies at the heart of all systematic inquiry.

Consider what a comparison between 'sane' and 'mad' families might well show: that the patterns of transaction inside the two sorts of family are in fact strikingly alike in many ways. Just as it is possible for Laing and Esterson to find evidence of parents exerting irreconcilable pressures on their mad children, so we might find analogous evidence of pressure on children who are sane. What do we then conclude? The crude answer is to throw the whole fabric of Laing and Esterson's argument out of the window. This, I am convinced, would be an error; for we can open up their argument and thereby improve it.

In the first place, we can reintroduce the traditional concern with predispositions. If some people buckle under the pressure of a double-bind and others do not, we can quite sensibly ask why. In attempting to answer this question, we find ourselves thinking about the fit between an individual's predispositions and the nature of the stress he faces – a more versatile frame of reference than either the Laingian one or the traditionally medical one it challenges. We also find ourselves wondering about differences in the reactions of mad and sane to such stress – differences in the way they think. These differences in their turn may give rise to vicious circles of mutual misunderstanding and distrust in 'mad' families that the 'sane' families manage to short-circuit.

It is here that we can use one of Laing's formulations to refine another. For Laing himself has often written as though he viewed insanity as the result of genuine sensitivity or openness to life's contradictions and brutalities, while sanity lay in our ability to insulate ourselves from these. When a sane man sees pictures of bombing and napalm, rape and humiliation, on the television, he is able to distance himself from these, treating them, in a sense, as though they were just pictures. The madman, in contrast, is open to these outrages and the suffering they are causing, as a matter of cold fact, to other people elsewhere in the world. When the sane man eats a beefburger, he eats a beefburger; when the madman does so, he is aware too of the cow that was slaughtered to make what he eats, the slaughter-house and the man who did the slaughtering. The sane man draws back from the logical implications of what he sees and does; the madman presses on relentlessly until his sense of horror deranges him. If Laing is right, and I strongly suspect that in this respect he is, we preserve our sanity, frequently, by the brusque curtailment of our imaginative powers.

Returning to the family and its double-binds, we can now foresee in what respects the responses of mad and sane may differ. The mad person enters with the full force of his imagination into the implications of what the double-binds suggest; the sane one will follow these implications for a while, but sooner or later he will draw back. Arbitrarily, he will disengage himself from the logical implications of his own train of thought.

One way of expressing this difference between mad and sane is to say that sanity depends on the blunting of our experience, or at least on its careful circumscription. Another less loaded way of making the same point – and one I find more congenial – is to say that sanity depends on a species of existential tact; on the willingness to engage oneself imaginatively, but only within certain bounds. Such tact springs, of course, from an adherence to social convention; but also from a sense of proportion – from an intuitive awareness of the chaos from which social conventions and rituals may frequently protect us.

We sometimes speak as though rationality were a simple and coherent virtue; but if the argument I have advanced here has any merit, it is clear that rationality makes demands on us that conflict. It is rational, in one sense, to follow a train of thought through to its logical conclusion. It is also rational to draw back from such trains of thought if they threaten to destroy our equilibrium. The first of these is a matter of intrinsic rationality; the second is the rationality of means and ends – the kind that requires us to make manoeuvres that are in themselves arbitrary or positively illogical, in order to preserve some longer-term objective.[3] Madness, on the present argument, results from an inability to maintain a balance between these two kinds of rationality – intrinsic rationality always being pursued at the expense of that of means and ends. In old-fashioned terms, madness consists in the tyranny of sensibility over sense.[4]

A virtue of this formulation is that it helps us overcome the squeamishness that writers like Laing convey about the notion of a cause. Enthusiasts for the phenomenological position frequently imply that such research renders the search for causes obsolete, but this must I think be a confusion arising from the equation of causal explanation with explanation that is reductive – with explaining away. For ideas can be causes just as much as genes and hormones are. And if the second of the three claims made about the double-bind is to mean anything, it must mean that it is the contradictory webs of meaning spun by parents around their children that *cause* their children to go mad. And such a claim is one, I would argue, that we can only examine by drawing comparisons.

If the second claim is precarious in this way, so too – for different reasons – is the third, about how the mad should be treated. For a long-standing and notorious difficulty in medical research is that knowledge of the causes of an illness often tells you little or nothing about how that illness might be cured. Laing might well reply that he is not concerned with cures but with human dignity and with the authenticity of experience. Yet it must surely remain true that madness leaves some people broken – a state in which the possibility of dignity and authenticity of experience are little consolation. And it must also be possible that the only resort, in attempting to prevent such wreckage of lives, may well be to drugs, or to some other form of physical treatment.

A further awkwardness of the purely transactional approach to madness is that it treats all the various manifestations of neurotic

3. Donald Winch has pointed out to me the parallel with Max Weber's (1968) distinction between *Wertrational* and *Zweckrational* – that is to say, between social action motivated by the pursuit of an ideal or 'value', and that motivated, more instrumentally, by considerations of ends and means.
4. The obverse pattern – the tyranny of means–ends rationality over the intrinsic – might well be said to characterize the psychopath; the person devoid of conscience, who can only think in terms of the effects he will produce.

and psychotic disability as equivalent.[5] This, I cannot help feeling, is a strategic error. Of the two young people I mentioned at the end of Chapter 3, for example, Daphne fits the transactional pattern closely: an excessively sensitive soul being driven out of her wits by her mother. Brian's on the other hand was a different story. He already inhabited a world of delusions that was alarmingly self-sufficient. And, revealingly, while one felt confident in using the term 'mad' about Brian, in Daphne's case I for one felt a strong impulse to hedge.

I do not in the least want to criticize thought that is unconventional or eccentric; but we cannot make sense of madness unless we are willing to discuss the extent to which an individual's thinking has become dislocated from the thinking that the rest of us are doing – either by becoming fragmented and hallucinatory, or by acquiring too powerful an internal coherence and autonomy. It is fashionable at the moment to suggest that the only requirement we can make of a body of thought is that it should be coherent in its own terms.[6] But it is precisely this quality of internal coherence that the fully fledged paranoiac of the psychiatric textbooks possesses; and we deny the strangeness of such thinking at our peril. (It was in the light of a paranoid vision, after all, that the Nazis recently committed genocide.) This is not a matter of thinking that is different from ours, it is one of thinking that is *mistaken* – of thinking that runs counter to our cumulative sense of what is literally, factually true. While this distinction is often disconcertingly awkward to draw – especially perhaps in academic life – and while it rarely excludes substantial doubt, it is one without which we are hopelessly at sea.[7]

We can now see that even the first of the three claims made on

5. On the other hand, work like Laing's does undermine the absurd psychiatric activity of coping with mental illness by coining more and more clinical categories with which to describe it.

6. See for instance Winch (1958), a position rightly dismissed by Quentin Skinner (1974a). There is also the suggestion that a concern with causes places an inquiry outside the hermeneutic tradition: see Taylor (1971). I cannot for the life of me see why this should be so.

7. Academic life provides the perfect refuge for the paranoid. Distinguished scholars and scientists frequently become obsessed with their own theories, and concern themselves only with what can be assimilated to these. It is easier as a consequence to envisage men on Mars than to contemplate certain academics changing their minds.

Laing and Esterson's behalf is more precarious than it seems. To justify the claim that someone's thinking is rational, we have to show that it is reasonably coherent with his perceptions and beliefs; that those perceptions and beliefs are themselves reasonably accurate; and that in pursuing his line of thought, the person is balancing intrinsic and means–ends considerations against one another in an adequate way. A paranoiac's thinking may well be rational in that it is coherent with his beliefs and perceptions, but irrational in that these beliefs and perceptions are inaccurate.[8] Likewise a schizophrenic's thinking may be accurately keyed to what is actually going on around him, yet lack coherence and 'tact'. So if we are to get down seriously to the business of relating sanity to rationality, we must show in what respects, and to what degrees, it is possible for someone to be coherent, accurate and 'tactful', yet mad; or, on the other hand, incoherent, inaccurate and 'tactless', yet sane. And until we have looked at the sane as well as the mad, we have no real idea of what standards of coherence, accuracy and 'tact' will pass muster. It is a matter not of being absolutely coherent or accurate, but reasonably or adequately so – and until we have made the required comparisons we cannot know what, in such a context, 'reasonably' or 'adequately' might mean.

Rather than playing the intellectually undemanding game of relativism in such matters, we would be better employed examining the conflicting functions that systems of ideas serve. And rather than examining those people who believe that, at every turn, the air they breathe is being poisoned by the Emperor Napoleon (or some other favoured power), it is worth thinking again for a moment about Isaac Newton. Newton offers us the paradigmatic instance of a man cut off from everyday realities by superbly constructed systems of thought. The first point to be grasped about him is that while some of his thinking was beautifully adapted to the requirements of physical science, the bulk of if was thinking of a mystical and even magical nature. He was

8. The paranoiac's 'tactlessness' may be great, but encapsulated with considerable finesse in the humbler systems of understanding on which daily competence depends. A man's inner life may be consumed by the belief that Genghis Khan is alive, well, living in South America, and influencing our thoughts. Yet in day-to-day transaction, little of this belief-system may show. The extent of such encapsulation among the sane and the mad, again, is something about which we still know relatively little.

deeply concerned with alchemy, and with the mysteries of the Trinity, and in comparison physics took up only a small proportion of his time.[9] He also underwent a mental collapse. In Keynes's words:

Somewhere about his fiftieth birthday on Christmas Day 1692, he suffered what we would now term a severe nervous breakdown. Melancholia, sleeplessness, fears of persecution – he writes to Pepys and to Locke and no doubt to others letters which lead them to think that his mind is deranged. He lost, in his own words, the 'former consistency of his mind'. He never again concentrated after the old fashion or did any fresh work. The breakdown probably lasted nearly two years, and from it emerged, slightly 'gaga', but still, no doubt, with one of the most powerful minds of England, the Sir Isaac Newton of tradition.[10]

His preoccupations with magic were forgotten, and he became 'the Sage and Monarch of the Age of Reason' – one of 'the principal sights of London for all visiting intellectual foreigners', among them Voltaire. In his day, such preoccupations with magic were acceptable, so the fact that we *now* see them as mistaken is largely irrelevant to the questions that, as psychologists, we wish to ask.[11] Altogether more pressing is the fact that his collapse turned him, at one blow, from a recluse into a public figure, and from being an undoubted genius to being, by his own exalted standard, burnt out.

Such events lead one to further uneasiness about the third of the claims around which this chapter is organized: the claim that it is by means of psychotic episodes that we reach greater authenticity of experience. This may sometimes happen, but in Newton's case one doubts it. 'Slightly "gaga"' was Keynes's phrase, and you fear that it was aptly applied.[12] Without question, mental collapse can bring us face to face with aspects of ourselves we had no idea were there. But in slicing away the layers of self-deception so drastically, we may well be slicing away a good deal else – notably our talents.

9. McGuire and Rattansi (1966).
10. Keynes (1951), p. 321.
11. Largely, but not entirely. It is worth noticing that it is t he mystical – and by implication more psychically 'dangerous' – aspects of his thought that dropped away after his collapse, and the 'safer' physics that remained.
12. It makes little sense, either, to think of a recluse like Newton being driven mad by a double-bind, for, except in fantasy, there was no one close enough to him to exert it.

The great landscape painter John Constable once wrote that without the occupation of painting 'my mind would soon devour me'. It may well be that Constable, Newton before his collapse, young Peter with his drawing in Chapter 5, and the rest of us – in varying ways, to differing degrees, and with differing amounts of self-knowledge – are all coping with the same predicament. We may all be using the systematic constructions of our minds in order to keep a sense of chaos at bay. That certainly is my suspicion; and for that reason, it is to the arts that I would now like to move.

14   Essential Tensions

In this last chapter, I want to pursue the idea of productive tension – the heart of the matter – looking at some of the balancing acts that painting, poetry and music demand of us.[1] One implication of the octagons was that works of art are symbolic devices that permit us temporarily to dissolve the boundary between the familiar and the alien – the 'I' and the 'not-I'. In playing these boundary games, however, we enter into relationships with the forces of discipline and constraint that are very complex indeed. It is these relationships that I want to explore.

In choosing artists to talk about, I have exercised a prejudice – in favour of work that conveys the sentiment of desire, and against that conveying horror. But as a preface, I have first to reinstate the notion of 'desire' itself, for at present this is still in some disgrace. In our attempts to live down our heritage of Victorian prudery about the physical expression of this emotion, we have tended to lapse into the 'Scandinavian Solution', generating a large rhetoric on the subject of sexuality, but in effect reducing it to a function as natural, and by implication as prosaic, as emptying our bladders. But to adopt this attitude is to cut ourselves off from the elaboration of perception and response that the acknowledgment of contradiction brings with it.[2] For sex fertilizes in more senses than the obstetric. In a phrase of Norman O. Brown's, 'sex becomes not only an object of thought

1. This is partly to counteract the tendency of recent research to exalt the scientist at the artist's expense. That science springs from a dialectical tension between 'conjecture and refutation' is now well-trodden ground: Kuhn (1962), (1970); and Lakatos and Musgrave (1970).
2. Symptomatically, Copenhagen's sex shops brim over with literal-minded portrayals of the perverse and ugly: solemn pyramids of men, women and monkeys, whips and vibrators. But you look in vain for Lucien Clergue's delightful photographs of his girlfriend in the sea; praised, rightly, by people as diverse as Picasso and Cocteau: Clergue (1970).

but in some sense an imaginative method of comprehension'.[3]
Like Freud, Brown here uses 'sex' as a conceptual label, approximately synonymous with the 'life instinct' or Eros: the appetite that leads us to preserve life and enrich it, to relate to others and have access to their experience. And this he contrasts with the 'death instinct' or Thanatos: the need to control others and to turn our knowledge of them, and of the world more generally, into something immutable.[4]

And conceptually, this opposition is of great significance, because it gives us the terms with which to grapple with the impulse that underlies the whole enterprise of art: namely, to petrify, to turn something living into something intransient – paint on a canvas, print on a page, music in a score.

Brown's books are, I find, profoundly invigorating to read. Rather than boring you, or making you feel inadequate, he spurs you on to think new thoughts and attempt new deeds. And he states the terms of the dialogue between Eros and Thanatos with brilliance, leaving you in no doubt as he does so that he backs the first against the second. Rather than 'controlled regression in the service of the ego', he advocates the 'active surrender of the controlling and deliberative mind': the abandonment of realistic, literal and commonsensical ways of thinking, and the pursuit of 'the meaning' that lies 'not in the words but between the words ... beyond the reach, the rape, of literal-minded explication'. He urges that we give up the 'reality-principle'; and give up the boundaries between 'inside and outside; subject and object; real and imaginary; physical and mental'. 'The conclusion of the whole matter,' he says, is to 'break down the boundaries, the walls. Down with defense mechanisms, character-armor; disarmament.'[5]

Even so, the position Brown takes up, especially in *Love's Body*, strikes me as unsatisfactory for two sorts of reason. He presupposes a bedrock of order that he does not fully acknowledge. (He is himself a classical scholar with a beautifully poised prose style, which it must have taken decades of discipline to perfect.) And he overlooks the extent to which, in exploring life's

3. Brown (1966), p. 249.
4. Eros stands here as a shorthand for the frame of mind associated with fixation in infancy; Thanatos for that associated with fixation during the latency period.
5. Brown (1966).

Erotic potentialities, we enter into a dialogue with the forces of order from which it would be self-destructive to escape. Where I have portrayed the permissive educator as wanting to slip away from this dialogue before it begins, Brown establishes it, pursues it for a while, but in the end slips away too. He rightly rejects the self-conscious rationality of the technologist, but offers in its place a view that is equally unacceptable – one that is in essence mystical.

The true nature of this dialogue is easiest to grasp if we begin with the question of technique. Here, an elementary knowledge of the arts comes to the psychologist's aid; a little knowledge, for example, of paintings and the ways in which they are produced. To look at all closely at a painting is continually to rediscover the same paradox: that our awareness of life's sensuous possibilities is enhanced by the transformation of something living into something still. A painting of any merit is not a slice of everyday experience, but a carefully wrought construction, sufficient in itself, that depends for its power over us on its creator's skill in manipulating the conventions and technical limitations of his medium. He works within these limitations, but searches continually for the alchemist's trick that will bring the image latent in his paint alive.

Moreover, the trick is one that should not come too easily. It is a lifetime's struggle with technical constraint that is formative of a vision beyond the merely facile. Take as an example, a landscape by Nicolas de Stael – one of the superb series he produced in the South of France in the early 1950s.[6] These pre-eminently are *paintings*: looking at them, you are inescapably conscious of the paint as a *substance*, and of the gestures with which it was laid on. The feats of sheer technique whereby areas of red, orange and violet paint are used to create a sense of a place that is now cool, but will soon be hot; and whereby the thick patches of paint, trowelled on to canvas, leave an impression of delicacy – these are what we return to over and again. But de Stael also refers us to the traditions of landscape painting, and to the prevailing conventions of abstract art; and it is by playing variations on these, as well as through his technical virtuosity, that he invades our sense of what a landscape is. Questions of tradition

6. Some are reproduced in Cooper (1961). A complete catalogue is provided by Chastel (1968).

and convention may at first sight seem remote from those of artistic sensibility; but only at first sight. The closer we move to an understanding of the work in question, the more clearly we grasp that complex games are being played: that the artist is weaving a cat's-cradle of intuitively perceptible references between at least three levels of meaning – that of tradition and stylistic convention, that of technique, and that of the image conveyed.

This interplay is often conspicuous in portrayal of the nude: for instance, Pierre Bonnard's memorable paintings, produced in the 1920s and 1930s, of his wife posed in and around her bath.[7] Like de Stael's landscapes, these owe much to painters' traditions – in this case that of the nude, passed down to us from the Ancient Greeks.[8] They capture some vital facet of our experience, and do so by playing upon the schemata that have governed the depiction of the human form for centuries. Again like de Stael, Bonnard appeals to us by the paradoxes of his technique. The form of the woman he portrays appears as partially diffused in the surrounding light. At the same time, especially when you notice the strange dryness of the paint surface, she looks like a stretch of landscape – not any landscape, but one of those that her husband habitually painted. These paradoxical sensations echo, in an odd and troubling way, what we know about the relationship of artist to model from which these works grew. We know, for instance, that Bonnard and his wife lived together in considerable seclusion, taking no part in the public polemics that did so much to inflate the reputation of his contemporary, Picasso. Bonnard was an *intimiste* both in his work and his style of life. On the other hand, his wife's preoccupation with bathing took on some of the properties of a neurotic ritual; and their life possessed little of the sensuous freedom of the paintings. Even in technique and working habits, Bonnard edged slowly towards his perception of an erotic ideal, rather than dashing off versions of it with a Picasso-like abandon. He tacked his canvases on to the wall of whatever rooms he happened to occupy; and fidgeted with them, a touch here and a touch there, often over a period of months or years. He is even said to have lurked in public gal-

7. See Plate 5. Some of the finest are reproduced in Fermigier's book.
8. Two who have written with distinction about such matters are Clark (1960) and Gombrich (1960). Also pertinent is Langer (1967).

leries, with his paints hidden, waiting his chance to retouch paintings of his that hung there.

Bonnard's, like de Stael's, are images that glow and vibrate; but they are, in the literal sense, dead. Not living, breathing women with their clothes off, nor beaches and sea: but inert areas of paint. Yet for those in their power, they are more vitally alive than any living woman, any landscape, except those one loves. And the strength of their appeal resides not just in their obvious beauty, but in their exploration of the ambiguities of life and death that our own sense of beauty rests upon.[9]

The same interlocking of opposites is clear in poetry; especially perhaps love poetry. Norman Brown rightly admires Rilke's poems; but these are nothing if not disciplined, and their imagery – in the famous sonnet about the unicorn and the virgin, for example – makes continual play with the imagery of life transfixed in a mirror.[10] The same verbal exactitude, and the same sense of paradox inform the best of more recent erotic poetry: for example, Denise Levertov's 'Song of Ishtar' – the Eastern goddess of fruitful increase:

> The moon is a sow
> and grunts in my throat
> Her great shining shines through me
> so the mud of my hollow gleams
> and breaks in silver bubbles
>
> She is a sow
> and I a pig and a poet
>
> When she opens her white
> lips to devour me I bite back
> and laughter rocks the moon
>
> In the black of desire
> we rock and grunt, grunt and
> shine[11]

A sense of sexual energy, almost alarming in its intensity, is contained here by an exactitude of word and rhythm; and the

9. There also exists a Marxist interpretation of this ambiguity: paintings being 'dead' in the sense that they are someone's loot – their property. John Berger (1972) argues for this view persuasively. Such petrification by ownership or patronage is, of course, different from that inherent to the act of painting itself; but is perfectly compatible with it.
10. See Hudson (1972).
11. Levertov (1964).

symbolism, too, is sharply dissonant – a pig-like greed and grunting set against the purity of the moon.

Even at the humdrum level of psychological tests – and there are few levels more so – memorable images would seem to flow when controlling and expressive impulses interact; though not when the intuition is allowed unedited rein. In the course of my own research, I have asked several hundred adolescents to make a drawing illustrative of the title 'Zebra Crossing'.[12] One gets street scenes by the score; pictures of zebras; even zebras crossing zebra crossings. Some are far-fetched; and, every now and again, one is beautifully drawn. But almost all of them were entirely unmemorable. Only one stands out in my recollection; and significantly, it was produced by an extremely convergent young man, and one with violently reactionary social and political attitudes. ('The most dangerous man in the world,' he offered, 'is the educated African.') Yet the drawing he produced, like his responses to the open-ended tests, positively bristled with a convoluted ingenuity: a diagrammatic representation of a three-legged, cross-Channel zebra race – an idea which was, in itself, a wry comment on another of my questions, about a false syllogism proving that every horse has three tails.[13]

On the same occasion I asked each boy to note down the names of the class-mates who struck him as especially hard-working, or widely read, or possessing certain interests. Under one or other of half a dozen headings, almost everyone cropped up at least once or twice. This young man was a rarity; though academically bright, he was mentioned by no one at all. A shy, touchy, defensive person, he used what he wrote and drew to establish a world in which he was, in a contrary way, a sovereign.

If the tension of Eros and Thanatos expresses itself in our products – humble or more lordly – it also does so, quite directly, in the life of the producer. Arguments about freedom, discipline and the Erotic mode come to roost, in other words, in the detailed study of the relation of the life to the work. And, particularly, in the study of those people given over, neck and crop, to the values the Erotic mode celebrates.

In his chapter on the 'Divided Self', in the *Varieties of Religious Experience*, William James has this to say:

12. There is a full description of those studies in Hudson (1966).
13. See Plate 6.

Some persons are born with an inner constitution which is harmonious and well balanced from the outset. Their impulses are consistent with one another, their will follows without trouble the guidance of their intellect, their passions are not excessive, and their lives are little haunted by regrets. Others are oppositely constituted . . . Their spirit wars with their flesh, they wish for incompatibles, wayward impulses interrupt their most deliberate plans, and their lives are one long drama of repentance and of effort to repair misdemeanours and mistakes.[14]

Somewhere between these two extreme types, the smoothly harmonious and the totally dissonant, lurks a race of people of special interest to us: those who can use the dissonant elements of their personalities as an energy source; and create memorable symbolic counterparts of this conflict for the rest of us to absorb.

There are thousands of biographies to choose from. I have chosen one from the world of jazz, and would like to devote a few pages to it, partly for reasons that are sentimental, and partly because apparent contradictions poke out at us from it at every level.[15]

Jazz was – and remains – pre-eminently an Erotic music; one that generates a sense of the dissolution of the boundary walls. Like any other, it is a world with its own iconography, and in its growth, one person stands in special eminence: Charlie Parker. He was notable in two ways. As a musician, he helped to alter jazz radically, carrying it a quantum step forward much as Corbusier carried architecture, or Einstein carried physics. He was also one of the first black Americans in public life to react to racial prejudice in its own terms: that is to say, by being unpleasant. To a younger generation of black militants, their political sensibilities sharpened and their musical ones blunted, Parker is now revered more as a social than as a musical revolutionary.

What kind of a person was he? The bare bones are clear enough.[16] Parker was born in Kansas City, in 1920, the only son of a mother who worked at night as a cleaner, and a father who

14. James (1960), p. 173.
15. To many of my generation, jazz was a liberation. Launched into a world of the middle way and the half measure, jazz stood for full-bloodedness – for going the whole hog.
16. I draw here on Russell's (1973) recent biography. Russell speaks with authority, having produced some of Parker's finest records (those on the Dial label). Williams' (1970) essays on this period are also useful.

was first a vaudeville performer and then a drifter. Like many black boys, he was indulged by his mother; but with no one to keep him in bed at night, he had by the age of twelve in effect dropped out of school; and ignoring the competent musical teaching provided by his high school, he began to hang around the clubs and brothels for which Kansas City was then famous.[17] There, he could listen to the best the world could offer – the Count Basie band, and saxophonists of towering gifts like Lester Young and Ben Webster.

By the age of fifteen, and learning by imitation, Parker was coming to grips with the vagaries of his own saxophone, and his ambition was hardening. He was also married for the first time, and a father. To make a reputation for himself he had to survive the ferocious rite of passage known as a jam session. There the tyros did their best to stay alive with the established musicians, and then listened while the great men were locked in battle one with the other. Parker's first sally into the arena ended in humiliation. Par for the course, in those days, was Coleman Hawkins' improvisation on 'Body and Soul'; and in attempting this Parker tried to break into double time. He failed and was ridiculed.

At this point, his biographer claims, Parker discovered that jazz could be played in different keys, not in the one all-purpose key of C. A fellow musician explained that there were twelve major keys; but rather than taking advice about which would be useful to him, he taught himself, unaided, to play certain tunes in all twelve – starting with C, then moving to D-flat, and so on. As Russell says, if genius is a capacity for taking infinite pains, it may also be a matter of taking the wrong course and arriving at a new destination; for Parker's contribution to jazz was to lie in the freedom of his harmonic invention.[18]

A year later, he hazarded another jam session, but was again humiliated. Using an old gramophone, he then set himself to copy Lester Young's solos until he had them note perfect. From insurance payments after a traffic accident, he bought a workable saxophone; and finding a band-leader he could trust, he learnt

17. Under the aegis of the notorious political boss Tom Pendergast, who reigned in Kansas City from the late 1920s until 1939.
18. Kansas City jazz was at that time played in C, B-Flat or F, it being rhythmically and melodically rather than harmonically inventive.

from him how to correct the rudimentary errors in his technique. As if crossing a threshold, Parker then passed, at the age of seventeen, from being a bumptious laughing-stock to being a musician who could be taken seriously.

By the time he was twenty, he was beginning to display the harmonic inventiveness, the speed, and the cutting tone that were to characterize the improvisations of his mature years. And he had moved to Harlem where he lived, in penury, for whatever music he could find. Including the mindless hours spent in dance bands of wretched quality, he had spent at this point in his career, Russell estimates, a minimum of 15,000 hours playing the saxophone. By the age of twenty-seven, he had become a heroin addict, had undergone a cure, and began to make those records of unchallengeable quality by which he is now known.

When, in his early thirties, he was once again in hospital he was assumed to be mad. The clinical report from New York's Bellevue Hospital speaks of 'high average intelligence, a hostile evasive personality, primitive and sexual fantasies associated with hostility, and gross evidence of paranoid thinking'. The diagnosis was one of 'acute alcoholism and undifferentiated schizophrenia' – and harking back to the difficulties of psychological measurement and evaluation examined in Chapter 3, we can only wonder at what that summing up might mean.

By the time he was thirty-four, Parker was dead. The doctor who examined the body guessed that his age must be somewhere between fifty and sixty. He had suffered stomach ulcers, pneumonia and cirrhosis of the liver; and he appeared to have had a heart attack. Physically, and in every other way, he died having 'pushed his fingers all the way into the glove'.

His life abounds with stories of outrage to the conventional decencies: he was unwilling, and perhaps unable, to be polite. One incident – at a club in Chicago – can stand for the rest:

Charlie finished a set and placed his horn on the top of the piano. Then he stepped off the bandstand, walked past the tables on the main floor, into the foyer, entered the pay telephone booth, closed the door, and proceeded to urinate on the floor. The yellow stream gushed forth as from a stallion, its pool dark and foaming as it spread under the door of the telephone booth and into the foyer. He came from the booth laughing. There was no explanation or apology.[19]

19. Russell (1973), p. 257.

Parker's life is one in which apparent paradoxes abound. The pampered child becomes capable of staggering feats of self-discipline; yet it seems that it was sheer hubris that led him to explore the harmonic structures that his contemporaries ignored. There is the sense, too, of a man whose impulses were, at one and the same time, fiercely channelled into music and allowed to spill over into every aspect of private gluttony. (The descriptions of him *eating* are among the most memorable in Russell's book.) A natural Bohemian, he none the less craved musical respectability, playing in front of string orchestras quite unsuited to him. There is also the strange pedagogical fact that a revolutionary stride was made on the basis of sedulous imitation, and of deadening hours of self-imposed practice: a training that should by rights have killed his capacity to improvise, but which set him free to become the 'magical machine-gunner' of his form.[20] Yet all this remains puzzling only as long as we refrain from a single imaginative leap: one that enables us to see his life flowing, in every detail, from the fertile tension between opposed demands and needs.

If the products of such tension are for the most part symbolic, the play of Eros and Thanatos upon one another can also take a very literal form indeed. In this century, the expectation of an early death among the artistically productive has been distressingly high. More or less directly, Charlie Parker killed himself. So did Nicolas de Stael – at the age of forty-one, just as he seemed to reach the full flood of his talent, he committed suicide.[21]

20. There are many other instances of direct imitation in jazz: the chain for example that links three tenor saxophonists – Coleman Hawkins to Ben Webster to Paul Gonsalves. The great British landscape-painter Turner is in this respect similar to Parker. A highly idiosyncratic revolutionary in paint, he made his name by technical mastery of conventional landscape drawing: Finberg (1961).

21. Attrition seems particularly fierce in the jazz world. Some of the greatest have lived into their sixties and seventies – Louis Armstrong, Duke Ellington, Coleman Hawkins – but many have not. Bix Beiderbecke, Charlie Christian, Eddie Lang, Clifford Brown and Fats Navarro all died in their twenties. Chu Berry, Herschel Evans, Wardell Gray, Parker himself, Bessie Smith and Fats Waller died in their thirties. And John Coltrane, Billie Holiday, Freddie Keppard, Bud Powell, Django Reinhardt and Art Tatum all died in their early to mid-forties. Lester Young almost made it to fifty, but not quite. Early death has also been frequent among poets: Dylan Thomas, Brendan Behan, Malcolm Lowry, John Berryman, Cesare Pavese, Randall Jarrell, Mayakovsky, Sylvia Plath. And apart from de Stael, among painters too: Modigliani, Gorki, Jackson Pollock, Mark Rothko. See Alvarez (1971).

This connection between mortality and artistic production lies at the centre of Elliott Jaques' excellent speculative essay, 'Death and the Mid-Life Crisis'.[22] Jaques noticed a historical tendency for those who work creatively to pass through a crisis in their mid- to late-thirties, this expressing itself in the shape of emotional upheaval, severe illness or even death. The mid-thirties are also associated, Jaques claims, with a change in an artist's style: before the mid-life crisis, a search for polished perfection of utterance; and after it, a new willingness to work spontaneously, because precious time is slipping by. Whether artistically gifted or not, it seems that most of us in middle-life come to our senses, realizing that time is short and that we are already in pawn. There is also the suggestion that, recently, the 'mid-life crisis' has shown signs of lingering on into the forties and fifties, presumably because we no longer have before us, as clearly defined social roles, the states of being young, mature and old.

This brush with the Reaper is deeply alarming, but liberating too. Arguably, in fact, we live in a state of falsity until this has taken place.[23] And what it liberates, Rollo May suggests, is the capacity not just to work in a particular style, but to express love and affection. In support, he quotes from a letter by his fellow psychologist, Abraham Maslow, who was at the time recovering from a heart attack:

My river has never looked so beautiful . . . Death, and its ever present possibility makes love, passionate love, more possible. I wonder if we could love passionately, if ecstasy would be possible at all, if we knew we'd never die.[24]

May goes on to argue that it is our inability, as a culture, to cope with old age, dying and death, that underlies our preoccupation with dissociated sexuality: the denial of death may thus carry with it the denial or distortion of desire.[25]

22. Jaques (1965). The 'mid-life crisis', again, is a focus of contemporary interest foreshadowed in the work of Jung. He saw the human biography in terms of 'metamorphoses', the central of these occurring at the 'turning of life', around thirty-five.
23. As Albert Camus has put it: 'There is only one liberty, to come to terms with death. After which anything is possible.'
24. May (1969), p. 99.
25. An interesting inference, one that May does *not* draw, is that the Christian ideal of life eternal may well have been adopted by Puritanical sects precisely because it renders the physical expression of love less likely!

The unity of these last chapters lies, then, in the belief that the pursuit of freedom becomes self-stultifying the moment it detaches itself from the processes of order. It seems that Eros and Thanatos are locked together in such a way that we cannot enjoy the first without submitting to the second. And although Brown's proclamation of the Erotic vision – of life before death – encourages us to look at the world of the artist, we realize as we do so the extent to which psychologists have neglected the 'death-like' properties that any worthwhile product of the imagination must have. It also forces us to acknowledge the extent to which human accomplishment follows from the exercise not of a single need, but from the skill we possess in reconciling needs and constraints that are in opposition.

And what is true of our products is true of the lives from which these flow. We all walk tight-ropes. To the mind trained to believe that causes and effects are arranged simply, in chains, this often seems baffling; a state of affairs that must somehow be changed. But once the step is taken, and we envisage ourselves as negotiators of conflicting forces, we cease to worry about whether we can squeeze each person into some simple interpretative box: mature or immature, mad or sane, convergent or divergent, reactionary or revolutionary. Instead, we set ourselves to identify what those conflicting needs are; and to trace their influence on the marbled configuration of each individual's life. Our task is not to dissolve contradictions, nor to explain them away, but to ferret out their nature and influence. Only achieve this, and we cease to shadow-box and begin to generate a body of understanding worthy of pursuit.

What will this understanding centre around? An image of the individual as someone whose grasp and whose needs continually evolve – who grows up and grows old – for the most part gradually, but always with the possibility of a sudden, catastrophic shift. And someone whose internal preoccupations are among the most potent determinants of the shape his own personal evolution takes. Caught up in the pursuit of fantasies as well as the more down-to-earth tactics of daily survival, he will gradually adopt the style by which others know him. And the progress he makes will in its turn be coloured, at least in part, by his perception of himself either as a victim of circumstance, or as an agent who is accountable for what he achieves.

And those achievements – what will they be? We have lapsed into the depressing assumption that men and women all claw their way up ladders of status, reaching for material rewards. But both in our private lives and in what we do more publicly we have the chance, now and again, to utter ourselves convincingly. We can take what floats around inside our heads, tantalizingly unformed, and offer it to those we care about as something sharply crystallized and committing – and this not because it makes us successful, nor even loved, but because it gives our longing a concrete expression. It is through this feat of eloquence that we become individuals; and it is with this singularly human gift that the psychologist must learn to come to terms.

References

ALTUS, W. D., 1970. 'Birth Order and its Sequelae', in *The Ecology of Human Intelligence*, ed. Liam Hudson (Harmondsworth: Penguin).

ALVAREZ, A., 1971. *The Savage God* (London: Weidenfeld & Nicolson).

ANASTASI, A., 1958. *Differential Psychology* (London: Macmillan).

ATKINS, E., 1973. Interview with Ronald Hayman in *The Times Saturday Review*, 24 February.

AUSTIN, M., 1971. 'Dream Recall and the Bias of Intellectual Ability', in *Nature*, 231, p. 59.

BANNISTER, D. and FRANSELLA, F., 1971. *Inquiring Man* (Harmondsworth: Penguin).

BARBER, T. X., 1969. *Hypnosis* (New York: Van Nostrand).

BARTLETT, F. C., 1932. *Remembering* (Cambridge University Press).

BERGER, J., 1972. *Selected Essays and Articles* (Harmondsworth: Penguin).

BERGER, P. L. and KELLNER, H., 1971. 'Marriage and the Construction of Reality', in *School and Society* (London: Routledge & Kegan Paul).

BERGIN, T. G. and FISCH, M. H., 1968. *The New Science of Giambattista Vico* (Ithaca: Cornell University Press).

BERNSTEIN, B., 1971. *Class, Codes and Control* (London: Routledge & Kegan Paul).

BLOOM, B. S., 1964. *Stability and Change in Human Characteristics* (New York: Wiley).

BOCK, R. D., 1973. 'Word and Image', *Psychometrika*, 38, p. 437.

BODMER, W. F., 1972. 'Race and I.Q.: the Genetic Background', in *Race, Culture and Intelligence*, ed. K. Richardson *et al.* (Harmondsworth: Penguin).

BORING, E. G., 1942. *Sensation and Perception in the History of Experimental Psychology* (New York: Appleton-Century-Crofts).

BOWERS, K. S., 1973. 'Situationism in Psychology', *Psychological Review*, 80, p. 307.

BRAGINSKY, B. M. and BRAGINSKY, D. D., 1974. *Mainstream Psychology* (New York: Holt, Rinehart & Winston).

BRONFENBRENNER, U., 1970. *Two Worlds of Childhood* (New York: Russell Sage Foundation).

BROWN, N. O., 1959. *Life against Death* (Wesleyan University Press).

BROWN, N. O., 1966. *Love's Body* (New York: Random House).

BRUNER, J., 1962. *On Knowing: Essays for the Left Hand* (Harvard University Press).

BUBER, M., 1958. *I and Thou* (New York: Scribner's).

BURT, C., 1961. 'Galton's Contribution to Psychology', *Bulletin of the British Psychological Society*, 45, p. 10.

BURT, C., 1962. Critical notice: 'Creativity and Intelligence', *British Journal of Educational Psychology*, 32, p. 292.

CARLSMITH, L., 1970. 'Effect of Early Father Absence on Scholastic Aptitude', in *The Ecology of Human Intelligence*, ed. Liam Hudson (Harmondsworth: Penguin).

CASEY, E. S., 1972. 'Freud's Theory of Reality', *Review of Metaphysics*, 25, p. 659.

CHASTEL, A., 1968. *Nicolas de Stael* (Paris: Le Temps).

CHOMSKY, N., 1970. 'Recent Contributions to the Theory of Innate Ideas', in *The Ecology of Human Intelligence*, ed. Liam Hudson (Harmondsworth: Penguin).

CLARK, K., 1960. *The Nude* (Harmondsworth: Penguin).

CLERGUE, L., 1970. *Née de la Vague* (London: Corgi).

COLEMAN, J. C., 1956. *Abnormal Psychology and Modern Life* (Glenview, Illinois: Scott Foresman).

COOPER, D., 1961. *Nicolas de Stael* (London: Weidenfeld & Nicolson).

CORMACK, M. and SHELDRAKE, P. F., 1974. 'Menstrual Cycle Variations in Cognitive Ability', *International Journal of Chronobiology*, 2, p. 53.

CRITCHLOW, K., 1969. *Order in Space* (London: Thames & Hudson).

DALTON, K., 1968. 'Ante-natal Progesterone and Intelligence', *British Journal of Psychiatry*, 114, p. 1377.

D'ANDRADE, R. G., 1970. 'Sex Differences and Cultural Institutions', in *The Ecology of Human Intelligence*, ed. Liam Hudson (Harmondsworth: Penguin).

DEWAN, E. M., 1967. 'On the Possibility of a Perfect Rhythm Method of Birth Control by Periodic Light Stimulation', *American Journal of Obstetrics and Gynaecology*, p. 1016.

DILTHEY, W., 1972. 'The Rise of Hermeneutics', *New Literary History*, 3, p. 229.

DOUGLAS, M., 1970. *Purity and Danger* (Harmondsworth: Penguin).

DRELLICH, M. G. and WAXENBERG, S. E., 1966. 'Erotic and Affectional Components of Female Sexuality', in *Sexuality of Women*, ed. J. H. Masserman (New York: Grune & Stratton).

EMERSON, J. P., 1970. 'Behaviour in Private Places', in *Recent Sociology No. 2*, ed. H. P. Dreitzel (New York: Macmillan).

ERIKSON, E. H., 1963. *Childhood and Society* (New York: Norton).

FARBER, L. H., 1966. *The Ways of the Will* (London: Constable).

FERMIGIER, A., no date. *Bonnard* (New York: Abrams).

FINBERG, A. J., 1961. *The Life of J. M. W. Turner, R.A.* (Oxford University Press).

FREUD, S., 1938. *General Introduction to Psychoanalysis* (New York: Garden City).

FROMM, E. and SHOR, R. E., 1972. *Hypnosis: Research Developments and Perspectives* (London: Elek).

GARDINER, P. (ed.), 1974. *The Philosophy of History* (Oxford University Press).

GARFINKEL, H., 1967. *Studies in Ethnomethodology* (Englewood Cliffs, N.J.: Prentice-Hall).

GEERTZ, C., 1973. *The Interpretation of Cultures* (New York: Basic Books).

GETZELS, J. W. and JACKSON, P. W., 1962. *Creativity and Intelligence* (New York: Wiley).

GETZELS, J. W. and JACKSON, P. W., 1970. 'Family Environment and Cognitive Style', in *The Ecology of Human Intelligence*, ed. Liam Hudson (Harmondsworth: Penguin).

GOFFMAN, E., 1959. *The Presentation of Self in Everyday Life* (New York: Doubleday).

GOMBRICH, E. H., 1960. *Art and Illusion* (London: Phaidon).

GOODENOUGH, D. R. *et al.*, 1973. *Repression, Interference and Field Dependence as Factors in Dream Forgetting*, Research Bulletin, Educational Testing Service, Princeton, October.

GOTTESMAN, I. I., 1968. 'Biogenetics of Race and Class', in *Social Class, Race and Psychological Development*, ed. M. Deutsch *et al.* (New York: Holt, Rinehart & Winston).

GREGORY, R. L., 1966. *Eye and Brain* (London: Weidenfeld & Nicolson).

GREVEN, P. J., 1973. *Child-Rearing Concepts, 1628–1861* (Itasca, Illinois: Peacock).

GUILFORD, J. P., 1959. 'Three Faces of Intellect', *American Psychologist*, 14, p. 469.

HABERMAS, J., 1972. *Knowledge and Human Interests* (London: Heinemann).

HADAMARD, J., 1945. *The Psychology of Invention in the Mathematical Field* (New York: Dover).

HALBERG, F., 1969. 'Chronobiology', *Annual Review of Physiology*, 31, p. 675.

HAMBURG, D. A. and LUNDE, D. T., 1967. 'Sex Hormones in the Development of Sex Differences in Human Behaviour', in *The Development of Sex Differences*, ed. E. E. Maccoby (London: Tavistock).

HAMPSHIRE, S., 1969. *Modern Writers and Other Essays* (London: Chatto & Windus).

HANSEN, S. and JENSEN, J., 1971. *The Little Red School-Book* (London: Stage One).

HEARNSHAW, L. S., 1964. *A Short History of British Psychology* (London: Methuen).

HENRY, J., 1966. *Culture against Man* (London: Tavistock).

HESSE, H., 1965. *Steppenwolf* (Harmondsworth: Penguin).

HILGARD, E. R., 1968. *The Experience of Hypnosis* (New York: Harcourt Brace & World).

HOLMES, M. A. M., 1973. *REM Sleep Patterning and Dream Recall in Convergers and Divergers*, Occasional Paper 16, Centre for Research in the Educational Sciences, Edinburgh University.

HOLMES, M. A. M., 1974. *The Academic Dispositions of Scientists and their Seasons of Birth*, Paper given to the Anabas Conference, Edinburgh University, March.

HOLT, R. R., 1967. 'Individuality and Generalisation in the Psychology of Personality', in *Personality*, ed. R. S. Lazarus and E. M. Opton (Harmondsworth: Penguin).

HUBEL, D. H., 1963. 'The Visual Cortex of the Brain', *Scientific American*, November.

HUDSON, L., 1960. 'A Differential Test of Arts/Science Aptitude', *Nature*, 186, p. 413.

HUDSON, L., 1961. *Arts/Science Specialisation*, Ph.D. dissertation, Cambridge University.

HUDSON, L., 1966. *Contrary Imaginations* (London: Methuen).

HUDSON, L., 1968. *Frames of Mind* (London: Methuen).

HUDSON, L., 1971. 'Intelligence, Race and the Selection of Data', *Race*, 12, p. 283.

HUDSON, L., 1972. *The Cult of the Fact* (London: Cape).

HUDSON, L., 1973a. 'Fertility in the Arts and Sciences', *Science Studies*, 3, p. 305.

HUDSON, L., 1973b. *Originality*, Oxford Biology Reader No. 60 (Oxford University Press).

HUDSON, L., 1973c. 'The Limits of Human Intelligence', in *The Limits of Human Nature*, ed. J. Benthall (London: Allen Lane).

HUDSON, L., 1975. 'The Traffic in Selves', *The Times Literary Supplement*, 24 February.

HUDSON, L. and JACOT, B., 1971. 'Marriage and Fertility in Academic Life', *Nature*, 229, p. 531.

HUDSON, L., JOHNSTON, J. and JACOT, B., 1972. *Perception and Communication in Academic Life*, Occasional Paper 8, Centre for Research in the Educational Sciences, Edinburgh University.

HUDSON, L., JACOT, B. and SHELDRAKE, P. F., 1973. *Lieben und Arbeiten: Patterns of Work and Patterns of Marriage*, Occasional Paper 12, Centre for Research in the Educational Sciences, Edinburgh University.

ISNARD, C. A. and ZEEMAN, E. C., 1974. 'Some Models from Catastrophe Theory in the Social Sciences', in *Uses of Models in the Social Sciences*, ed. L. Collins (London: Tavistock).

JAMES, W., 1960. *The Varieties of Religious Experience* (London: Fontana).

JAQUES, E., 1965. 'Death and the Mid-Life Crisis', *International Journal of Psychoanalysis*, 46, p. 502.

JENSEN, A. R., 1969. 'How Much Can We Boost I.Q. and Scholastic Achievement?', *Harvard Educational Review*, 39, p. 1.

JONES, E., 1961. *The Life and Work of Sigmund Freud*, ed. L. Trilling and S. Marcus (London: Hogarth).

JOURARD, S. M., 1964. *The Transparent Self* (New York: Van Nostrand).

JOYCE, C. R. B. (ed.), 1971. *Psychopharmacology* (London: Tavistock).

JOYCE, C. R. B., 1972. 'Can Drugs affect Personality?', in *Some Myths of Human Biology* (London: BBC Publications).

KAGAN, J., 1970. 'On the Need for Relativism', in *The Ecology of Human Intelligence*, ed. Liam Hudson (Harmondsworth: Penguin).

KELLY, G. A., 1955. *The Psychology of Personal Constructs* (New York: Norton).

KEYNES, J. M., 1951. *Essays in Biography* (London: Hart-Davis).

KINSEY, A. C. *et al.*, 1948. *Sexual Behaviour in the Human Male* (Philadelphia: Saunders).

KINSEY, A. C. *et al.*, 1953. *Sexual Behaviour in the Human Female* (Philadelphia: Saunders).

KLEIN, V., 1966. 'The Demand for Professional Womanpower', *British Journal of Sociology*, 17, p. 183.

KUHN, T. S., 1962. *The Structure of Scientific Revolutions* (Chicago University Press).

KUHN, T. S., 1970. 'The Essential Tension', in *The Ecology of Human Intelligence*, ed. Liam Hudson (Harmondsworth: Penguin).

LAING, R. D., 1960. *The Divided Self* (London: Tavistock).

LAING, R. D., 1961. *The Self and Others* (London: Tavistock).

LAING, R. D., 1967. *The Politics of Experience* (Harmondsworth: Penguin).

LAING, R. D., 1970. *Knots* (London: Tavistock).

LAING, R. D. and ESTERSON, A., 1964. *Sanity, Madness and the Family* (London: Tavistock).

LAING, R. D., PHILLIPSON, H. and LEE, A. R., 1966. *Interpersonal Perception* (London: Tavistock).

LAKATOS, I. and MUSGRAVE, A. (eds.), 1970. *Criticism and the Growth of Knowledge* (Cambridge University Press).

LANGER, S., 1967. *Mind: an Essay on Human Feeling* (Johns Hopkins University Press).

LARKIN, P., 1964. *The Whitsun Weddings* (London: Faber).

LEISHMAN, J. (trans.), 1949. *Sonnets to Orpheus*, by Rilke (London: Hogarth).

LESSING, D., 1966. *A Proper Marriage* (London: Panther).

LEVERTOV, D., 1964. *O Taste and See* (New York: New Directions).

LEVY-AGRESTI, J. and SPERRY, R. W., 1968. 'Differential Perceptual Capacities in Major and Minor Hemispheres', *Proceedings of the National Academy of Science*, 61, p. 1151.

LEWIS, I. M., 1971. *Ecstatic Religion* (Harmondsworth: Penguin).

LOMAS, P., 1973. *True and False Experience* (London: Allen Lane).

LORENZ, K., 1966. *On Aggression* (London: Methuen).

LURIA, A. R., 1969. *The Mind of a Mnemonist* (London: Cape).

MCCARTHY, M., 1943. *The Company She Keeps* (London: Weidenfeld & Nicolson).

MCCARTHY, M., 1956. *A Charmed Life* (London: Weidenfeld & Nicolson).

MCCLELLAND, D. C., 1961. *The Achieving Society* (New York: Van Nostrand).

MCCLELLAND, D. C., 1970. 'On the Psychodynamics of Creative Physical Scientists', in *The Ecology of Human Intelligence*, ed. Liam Hudson (Harmondsworth: Penguin).

MCGUIRE, J., 1974. *Birth Order and Cognitive Style*, Unpublished Research Paper, Research Unit on Intellectual Development, Edinburgh University.

MCGUIRE, J. E. and RATTANSI, P. M., 1966. 'Newton and the "Pipes of Pan"', *Notes and Records of the Royal Society of London*, 21, p. 108.

MCHUGH, P., 1968. *Defining the Situation* (Indianapolis: Bobbs-Merrill).

MAILER, N., 1974. *Marilyn* (New York: Grosset & Dunlap).

MANIS, J. G. and MELTZER, B. N., 1967. *Symbolic Interaction* (Boston, Mass.: Allyn & Bacon).

MARCUSE, H., 1955. *Eros and Civilisation* (Boston, Mass.: Beacon).

MASTERS, W. H. and JOHNSON, V. E., 1966. *Human Sexual Response* (Boston, Mass.: Little, Brown).

MAY, R., 1969. *Love and Will* (New York: Norton).

MEDAWAR, P. B., 1967. *The Art of the Soluble* (London: Methuen).

MELZACK, R., 1973. *The Puzzle of Pain* (Harmondsworth: Penguin).

MERLEAU-PONTY, M., 1962. *Phenomenology of Perception* (London: Routledge & Kegan Paul).

MILGRAM, S., 1970. 'Behavioural Study of Obedience', in *The Ecology of Human Intelligence*, ed. Liam Hudson (Harmondsworth: Penguin).

MILGRAM, S., 1974. *Obedience to Authority* (London: Tavistock).

MILLER, G. A. *et al.*, 1960. *Plans and the Structure of Behaviour* (New York: Holt, Rinehart & Winston).

MISCHEL, T. (ed.), 1969. *Human Action* (New York: Academic).

MOLINARI, S. and FOULKES, D., 1969. 'Tonic and Phasic Events during Sleep', *Perceptual and Motor Skills*, 29, p. 343.

MONEY, J. *et al.*, 1957. 'Imprinting and the Establishment of Gender Role', *Archives of Neurological Psychiatry*, 77, p. 333.

MONEY, J., 1970. 'Genetic Abnormality and Intelligence', in *The Ecology of Human Intelligence*, ed. Liam Hudson (Harmondsworth: Penguin).

MONOD, J., 1972. *Chance and Necessity* (London: Collins).

NEILL, A. S., 1968. *Summerhill* (Harmondsworth: Penguin).

ORNE, M. T., 1959. 'The Nature of Hypnosis', *Journal of Abnormal and Social Psychology*, 58, p. 277.

OSGOOD, C. E. and LURIA, Z., 1954. 'A Blind Analysis of a case of Multiple Personality using the Semantic Differential', *Journal of Abnormal and Social Psychology*, 49, p. 579.

OSGOOD, C. E. *et al.*, 1957. *The Measurement of Meaning* (Urbana: University of Illinois Press).

PIAGET, J., 1932. *The Moral Judgment of the Child* (New York: Harcourt Brace).

POLANYI, M., 1966. *The Tacit Dimension* (London: Routledge & Kegan Paul).

POLANYI, M., 1973. *Personal Knowledge* (London: Routledge & Kegan Paul).

POMEROY, W. B., 1967. 'The Masters–Johnson Report and the Kinsey Tradition', in *An Analysis of Human Sexual Response*, ed. R. and E. Brecher (London: Deutsch).

POPPER, K. R., 1972. *Objective Knowledge: an Evolutionary Approach* (Oxford University Press).

PROUST, M., 1966. *Swann's Way, Part 2* (London: Chatto & Windus).

RAPOPORT, R. N. and RAPOPORT, R. V., 1969. 'The Dual Career Family', *Human Relations*, 22, p. 3.

RICHARDS, M. P. M. (ed.), 1974. *The Integration of a Child into a Social World* (Cambridge University Press).

RICHARDSON, K. *et al.* (eds.), 1972. *Race, Culture and Intelligence* (Harmondsworth: Penguin).

ROAZEN, P., 1975. *Freud and His Followers* (New York: Knopf).

ROBINSON, P. A., 1969. *The Sexual Radicals* (London: Paladin).

ROE, A., 1953. 'A Psychological Study of Eminent Psychologists and Anthropologists and a comparison with Biological and Physical Scientists', *Psychological Monographs*, 67, No. 352.

RUSSELL, B., 1967. *The Autobiography of Bertrand Russell 1872–1914* (London: Allen & Unwin).

RUSSELL, R., 1973. *Bird Lives* (London: Quartet).

RYCROFT, C. (ed.), 1968. *Psychoanalysis Observed* (Harmondsworth: Penguin).

RYCROFT, C., 1971. *Reich* (London: Fontana).

RYLE, G., 1949. *The Concept of Mind* (London: Hutchinson).

SACKS, O., 1972. 'The Great Awakening', *Listener*, p. 521, 26 October.

SACKS, O., 1973. *Awakenings* (London: Duckworth).

SARTRE, J.-P., 1970. 'Intentionality: a Fundamental Idea in Husserl's Phenomenology', *Journal of the British Society for Phenomenology*, 1, p. 4.

SEXTON, V. S. and MISIAK, H., 1971. *Historical Perspectives in Psychology* (Belmont, Calif.: Wadsworth).

SHELDRAKE, P. F. and TURNER, B., 1973. 'Perceptions and factions in a Therapeutic Community', *Human Relations*, 26, p. 371.

SHOTTER, J., 1973. 'Prolegomena to an understanding of Play', *Journal for the Theory of Social Behaviour*, 3, p. 47.

SIEGEL, S., 1956. *Nonparametric Statistics* (New York: McGraw-Hill).

SILVERMAN, S. M. (in press). 'Parental Loss and Scientists', *Science Studies*.

SKINNER, B. F., 1948. *Walden Two* (New York: Macmillan).

SKINNER, B. F., 1972. *Beyond Freedom and Dignity* (London: Cape).

SKINNER, Q., 1974a. ' "Social Meaning" and the Explanation of Social Action', in *The Philosophy of History*, ed. P. Gardiner (Oxford University Press).

SKINNER, Q., 1974b. 'Some Problems in the Analysis of Political Thought and Action', *Political Theory*, 2, p. 277.

SPERRY, R. W., 1964. 'The Great Cerebral Commissure', *Scientific American*, January.

SPIRO, M. E., 1956. *Kibbutz: Venture in Utopia* (Harvard University Press).

STOLLER, R. J., 1968. *Sex and Gender* (London: Hogarth).

STERN, K., 1966. *The Flight from Woman* (London: Allen & Unwin).

STORR, A., 1972. *The Dynamics of Creation* (London: Secker & Warburg).

STORR, A., 1973. *Jung* (London: Fontana).

STRAUSS, A., 1969. *Mirrors and Masks* (San Francisco: Sociology Press).

STURUP, G. K., 1971. 'Sex Offenders in Denmark', in *Personality and Science*, ed. I. T. Ramsey and R. Porter (Edinburgh Churchill Livingstone).

SULLOWAY, F., 1972. *The Role of Cognitive Flexibility in Science*, unpublished paper, Department of History of Science, Harvard University, October.

SZASZ, T., 1962a. *The Myth of Mental Illness* (London: Secker & Warburg).

SZASZ, T., 1962b. 'The Concept of Transference', *International Journal of Psychoanalysis*, 44, p. 432.

TART, C. T. (ed.), 1969. *Altered States of Consciousness* (New York: Wiley).

TAYLOR, C., 1971. 'Interpretation and the Sciences of Man', *Review of Metaphysics*, 25, p. 3.

THIGPEN, C. H. and CLECKLEY, H. A., 1957. *The Three Faces of Eve* (London: Secker & Warburg).

THORNDIKE, R. L., 1963. 'Some Methodological Issues in the Study of Creativity', *Proceedings of the 1962 Invitation Conference on Testing Problems*, Educational Testing Service, Princeton.

TIGER, L. and FOX, R., 1972. *The Imperial Animal* (London: Secker & Warburg).

TRILLING, L., 1954. *The Liberal Imagination* (New York: Doubleday Anchor).

VALLANTIN, A., 1954. *Einstein* (London: Weidenfeld & Nicolson).

VERNON, P. E., 1961. *The Structure of Human Abilities* (London: Methuen).

VERNON, P. E., 1969. *Intelligence and Cultural Environment* (London: Methuen).

WALLACH, M. A. and KOGAN, N., 1965. *Modes of Thinking in Young Children* (New York: Holt, Rinehart & Winston).

WANN, T. W. (ed.), 1964. *Behaviourism and Phenomenology* (Chicago University Press).

WARD, C. D. *et al.*, 1973. 'Birth Order and Dreams', *Journal of Social Psychology*, 90, p. 155.

WATSON, J. B., 1913. 'Psychology as the Behaviourist Views It', *Psychological Review*, 20, p. 158.

WEBB, E. J. *et al.*, 1966. *Unobtrusive Measures* (Skokie, Illinois: Rand McNally).

WEBER, M., 1930. *The Protestant Ethic and the Spirit of Capitalism* (New York: Scribner's).

WEBER, M., 1968. *Economy and Society*, ed. G. Roth and C. Wittich (New York: Bedminster Press).

WEINBERG, S. K., 1955. *Incest Behaviour* (Secancus, N.J.: Citadel).

WENDT, H. W., 1973. *Early Circannual Rhythms and Adult Human Behaviour*, Paper presented to the XIth Conference of the International Society for Chronobiology, Hanover, July.

WHYTE, L. L., 1962. *The Unconscious before Freud* (London: Tavistock).

WILLIAMS, M., 1970. *The Jazz Tradition* (Oxford University Press).

WILLIAMS, R. J., 1963. *Biochemical Individuality* (New York: Wiley).

WILSON, A., 1967. *No Laughing Matter* (London: Secker & Warburg).

WINCH, P., 1958. *The Idea of a Social Science* (London: Routledge & Kegan Paul).

WINCH, R. F., 1963. *The Modern Family* (New York: Holt, Rinehart & Winston).

WINNICOTT, D. W., 1964. *The Child, the Family, and the Outside World* (Harmondsworth: Penguin).

YOUNG, W. C., GOY, R. and PHOENIX, C., 1964. 'Hormones and Sexual Behaviour', *Science*, 143, p. 212.

ZANGWILL, O. L., 1970. 'The Consequences of Brain Damage', in *The Ecology of Human Intelligence*, ed. Liam Hudson (Harmondsworth: Penguin).

ZANGWILL, O. L., 1972. ' "Remembering" Revisited', *Quarterly Journal of Experimental Psychology*, 24, p. 123.

ZANGWILL, O. L., 1974. 'Consciousness and the Cerebral Hemispheres', in *Hemisphere Function in the Human Brain*, ed. S. J. Dimond and J. G. Beaumont (London: Elek).

ZEEMAN, E. C., 1971. 'The Geometry of Catastrophe', *The Times Literary Supplement*, 10 December.

Index

PSYCHOLOGY

A DICTIONARY FOR DREAMERS Tom Chetwynd 95p
A comprehensive key to the baffling language of dream symbolism.
Over 500 archetypal symbols give essential clues to understanding
the ingeniously disguised, life-enriching, often urgent messages to
be found in dreams.

THE MANUFACTURE OF MADNESS Thomas S. Szasz £1.75
'In the past, man created witches; now he creates mental patients.'
A comprehensive study of Inquisition and the psychiatric
establishment. A highly controversial and persuasive work.

THE MYTH OF MENTAL ILLNESS Thomas S. Szasz £1.50
'I submit that the traditional definition of psychiatry, which is still
in vogue, places it alongside such things as alchemy and astrology
and commits it to the category of pseudo-science.' *Thomas Szasz*.
The book that rocked the psychiatric establishment.

PSYCHIATRY AND ANTI-PSYCHIATRY
David Cooper 50p
A radical social re-evaluation of the whole concept of 'madness' and
a new approach to the psychological problems of personal
relationships from one of Britain's leading radical psychiatrists.

STEPS TO AN ECOLOGY OF MIND
Gregory Bateson £2.50
This book develops a new way of thinking about the nature of
order and organisation in living systems, a unified body of theory
so encompassing and interdisciplinary that it illuminates all areas of
study of behaviour and biology.

CRIME AND PERSONALITY H. J. Eysenck £1.25
A revised edition of the controversial and classic study of intelligence,
genes and aberration.

HUMAN BEINGS Liam Hudson £2.50
Liam Hudson's study of human psychology is readable, accessible
and sensible. This is a book about ourselves – our dreams, our
fears, our triumphs, disasters and experiments.

COUNTER CULTURE

THE DYADIC CYCLONE
John C. Lilly and Antonietta Lilly   £1.50
A deeper journey into the interior of the mind. John and
Antonietta Lilly describe their dyadic relationship and Lilly includes
his theories on the intelligence of dolphins in this latest,
revolutionary work.

DRUGS OF HALLUCINATION   Sidney Cohen   60p
A lucid account of the discovery and first synthesis of LSD, its
use and dangers in experimental psychiatry and self-induced
transcendental experiences.

THE FEMALE EUNUCH   Germaine Greer   75p
The book that caused a revolution, the central focus of the
Women's Liberation movement.

FOLK DEVILS AND MORAL PANICS   Stan Cohen   50p
Teddy Boys, Mods and Rockers, Hell's Angels, football hooligans,
Skinheads, student militants, drugtakers: these are the folk devils
of our time. A classic study of deviancy sociology. Illustrated.

ORIENTAL MAGIC   Idries Shah   50p
With a wealth of illustrations that include spells, invocations,
curses, ceremonies, rituals, talismans and rites, this is an
encyclopaedic enquiry into the world of the Eastern occult.

PEOPLE TOGETHER   Clem Gorman   90p
A guide, handbook, and history of communal living in a 1970s
British context.

PLAY POWER   Richard Neville   50p
'The best work yet on what, in pleasanter days, used to be called
the Love Generation.' ROLLING STONE. This is what it was all about.

THE PROSTITUTION PAPERS   Kate Millett   50p
The prostitute is the archetypal exploited 'woman as object' – an
intense and arresting series of dialogues with New York prostitutes
by one of the leading figures in Women's Liberation.

WITHOUT MARX OR JESUS   Jean-François Revel   50p
The new American revolution has begun. It offers the only
possible escape for mankind today – the acceptance of
technological civilisation as a means and not an end.

SOCIOLOGY

THE WILD BOY OF AVEYRON   Harlan Lane   £1.95
The true story of a nine year old boy found living wild in the woods
outside Paris and of the attempts of a brilliant and enlightened
surgeon to 'civilise' him. The work of Itard was, and is, influential
in the education of deaf and dumb children.

PEOPLE TOGETHER   Clem Gorman   90p
A guide, handbook, and history of communal living in a 1970s
British context.

THE PROSTITUTION PAPERS   Kate Millett   50p
The prostitute is the archetypal exploited 'woman as object' – an
intense and arresting series of dialogues with New York prostitutes
by one of the leading figures in Women's Liberation.

BREAKDOWN   Stuart Sutherland   £1.25
One man's harrowing account of his own nervous collapse, the
treatment he received and its effects. This is followed by a full
evaluation of the merits and demerits of various kinds and systems
of therapy.

THE SOCIAL PHILOSPHERS   Robert Nisbet   £2.50
This provocative absorbing essay in social and intellectual history
shows that Western social philosophy has been preoccupied with
man's perennial quest for community: military, religious,
revolutionary, ecological and plural.

STEPS TO AN ECOLOGY OF MIND
Gregory Bateson   £2.50
This book develops a new way of thinking about the nature of
order and organisation in living systems, a unified body of theory
so encompassing and interdisciplinary that it illuminates all areas of
study of behaviour and biology.

SUBURBIA   David Thorns   60p
Is the suburb the successful fusion of town and country or a
mirror of the most depressing features of urban existence? A
critical analysis of the origin and components of suburbia.

WITHOUT MARX OR JESUS   Jean-François Revel   50p
The new American revolution has begun. It offers the only possible
escape for mankind today – the acceptance of technological
civilisation as a means and not an end.

A SONG FOR EVERY SEASON   Bob Copper   £1.25
A year in the life of a Sussex farming family . . . their work, their
traditions and above all their music and their songs.

LINGUISTICS AT LARGE   Noel Minnis   75p
Linguistics: a semantic jungle or a valuable key to the problems of
sociology, anthropology, education, literary criticism and
psychology? Fourteen lectures presented to the ICA.

MYTHOLOGIES   Roland Barthes   75p
An entertaining and elating introduction to the science of
semiology – the study of the signs and signals through which
society expresses itself, from the leading intellectual star.

*All these books are available at your local bookshop or newsagent, or can be
ordered direct from the publisher. Just tick the titles you want and fill in the
form below.*

Name ....

Address ....

....

Write to Paladin Cash Sales, PO Box 11, Falmouth, Cornwall TR10 9EN
Please enclose remittance to the value of the cover price plus:

UK: 18p for the first book plus 8p per copy for each additional book
ordered to a maximum charge of 66p

BFPO and EIRE: 18p for the first book plus 8p per copy for the next 6
books, thereafter 3p per book

Overseas: 20p for first book and 10p for each additional book

*Granada Publishing reserve the right to show new retail prices on covers, which
may differ from those previously advertised in the text or elsewhere.*